The Diary Of
A Self-Taught
Make Up Artist

Elinah Success Mangena

TABLE OF CONTENTS

DEDICATION

To my family
Mr & Mrs Mangena
Mr & Mrs Ndebele
Miss Maphosa
Lamlela
Thulani
Nqobizitha
Ancillar
Arnold
Nqgabutho
Pauline
Katriona
Andile
Sibongile
Moses
Zimkhitha

God you have seen me through it, He know my end from the beginning.

Psalm 9 vs 1 I will give thanks to you, Lord, with all my heart; I will tell of all your wonderful deeds.

ACKNOWLEDGEMENTS

Lord l acknowledge your hand upon my life and your Mighty works, may I never think highly of myself and forget the one who has enabled me. Thank you for being faithful, never giving up on me, and always showing up at the right time.

I wanted to extend my humble appreciation to my family, brothers, sisters, mothers, and fathers. Each one of you has contributed to the woman I have become. To my mum and dad, thank you for doing your best in raising me and naming me Elinah, meaning "shining light" I hope I have become that to you. To my brother Nqobizitha, you have played an enormous role in my life; you have been my pastor, friend, therapist, and graphic designer. On my birthday, you wrote me a love letter, *"on this day many years ago, God blessed us with a mother, aunt, sister, and a BossLady. I am a proud brother today, not just because of her birthday but because she always had a strong character like our mum, she has that philanthropic heart like mum, and she is a Bosslady and my sister."* Ancillar, thank you for pushing me to pursue this gift to its full capacity."

To my second family, my friends (Henrietta Chatambudza, Thembie "Ntie" Phieda, Ayanda "Nda" Dube, Tsitsi "Doc" and Sandie) you have all come into my life at different times and became my "Aaron and Hur," when others despised me, lied about me, looked down on me, you held me up. You know all my strengths and weaknesses, but you still chose me to be your friend. You are academics, creatives, prayer warriors, comedians, and professional dancers; you certainly brighten up my life.

To my Business mentor Mr. Nkomo, you always shared your knowledge, wisdom, and time. Remember the first business idea I had, "Buds & Bloom," you took time from your day, sat down, created a business profile, financial plan, etc.; even though it never got off the ground, you never gave up on me. I will never forget your words, "to be successful, you have to invest in yourself; you must read a book each day even if it's just a page." "Don't allow people to hold so much power over you, expect people to help or break you, just be prepared for both"

To Novuyo Sithole, my first roommate, thank you for seeing that girly girl in me and bringing her out; if it weren't for you, I would still be the Vaseline and green bar soap girl (not that there is anything wrong with that). I am your little sister, the only person that calls me (Stamina).

To my spiritual parents, your prayers have propelled me to go through challenges and come out victorious. You continue to admonish me when necessary, open your home when I needed shelter and a sense of hope and belonging.

To my clients, you are the reason why I get to work and enjoy it. I am so grateful for the pleasure of serving you, the trust you have placed in me; because of your loyalty and referrals, my business is growing so fast. I take what I do as a ministry; I pray for you and value you greatly. You have shared your homes, food, and time with me. I have learned a great deal from your experiences, and I treasure them. I have the pleasure of having the front row seat at your special moments; thank you.

To my family on Instagram, Facebook, Tok-Tok, and YouTube, we share a special bond; for most, we haven't met, but your support has been amazing; you show and express your love for me like your very own sister. Every post share, like, comment and referral have hugely contributed to my journey as an Award Winner Makeup Artist. May the seeds you have planted in my life produce good fruit in the areas of your life that need fruitfulness. Cheers to growing together.

To each person who has touched my life in any way, you have made me the woman I am today. May you look at me and see your contribution and how it has positively affected my life and those I have impacted and I hope I have represented you well and are proud of me. I pray I will have the opportunity to do the same for you and your children and those connected to you.

FOREWORD

I first made contact with Elinah Success Mangena in 2014. In my time of ministry I have some girls who are just persistent with the pursuit. They follow after and do not let go. Elinah is one of them and the journey has been incredible. I felt her energy and drive for life and had a strong desire to go on the journey with her. This book is indeed a dramatic reveal of this journey.

As I read the book, my mind was enthralled by what the Lord had done in Elinah's life. My heart was filled with emotion and vivid images of the struggles she has had to go through to achieve her vision, a picture of the millions of young people searching for greener pastures. As pastors, my husband and I have worked with hundreds of young people that have stepped out in faith to get their dreams going. But, Elinah has been exceptional because of her tenacity and drive to succeed. She has been through so much and been on the brink of death, but her fighting spirit has kept her going in spite of the circumstances she found herself in.

I have had the opportunity to share faith and encouragement with her, and I have seen her respond and rise to new passion and energy levels. What you will read in this book will inspire you to press on against all odds. You will learn to innovate and turn hopeless situations into amazing tapestries of success, creativity, and destiny.

Elinah decided to push herself into something beyond her natural ability. Over the years, she has become a phenomenal makeup artist and has become a coach, mentor, pastor, "mom" to many young ladies whose destinies have been provoked by this amazing story.

As you read this book, may your faith be ignited to burn brightly in the next season of your life. May you be inspired to live a life that goes beyond just your life, just as Elinah has chosen to be a blessing to many. May your life become a blessing to someone else. May your success cause others to pursue their dreams

Congratulations, girl, you have earned your name amongst the great. You have been focused on pursuing your vision, and as Dr. Tich says, you have become "Beyond Extraordinary. This is the beginning; go after every dream, exercise Crazy Faith, and change the world. You are an amazing daughter.

Let's start a movement that shall cause many to come out of failure and rediscover dreams that had been put away. One day your story shall be a book that shall be read by millions of people. Begin your diary today.

God bless you

Dr. Princisca
Author, publisher, thought leader, change agent, and mum.
FaithLife, Success Paradigms 101, Faithland Publishers

INTRODUCTION

I am an example of a late bloomer; Richard Karlgaard once wrote, *"So what exactly does it mean to be a late bloomer? Simply put, a late bloomer is a person who fulfills their potential later than expected; they often have talents that aren't visible to others initially. They usually achieve their potential in novel and unexpected ways, surprising even those closest to them, even though they are not attempting to impress them. The expectations of parents or society are a false path that leads to burnout and brittleness, or even to depression and illness. Late bloomers are those who find their supreme destiny on their own schedule, in their own way"*. I am sure some are reading this statement and can relate to it just like me. In my early twenties, I had barely found my path, where exactly am going, and how am getting there.

It all seemed that all my age mates had found their path, stable careers, stable relationships, own apartments, and buying cars. It was frustrating at times because I had set goals for myself that I would have accomplished a couple of things by the age of twenty-five, certainly in the area of career path and marriage (FYI, I am still not married, but I will get married). You might conclude that's the end of it, while it is just the beginning. This book will serve as an encouragement to those who feel like it's too late to start a business, go back to school, change careers, learn a new skill, find your purpose, and pursue it; I believe that success can happen at any time and at any age when you apply the correct principles.

"A little one shall become a thousand, and a small one
a strong nation: I the LORD will hasten it in his time."
Isaiah 60:22 KJV

"When the time is right, I, the Lord, will make it happen."

Every time I detect impatience in myself, I go back to the above scripture. God doesn't say when you cry when you pray or fast when we give when we study, But "when the time is right." There is the "time" of God that comes to our lives; wait for it. Any activity, principles, and statutes from the Bible that we are encouraged to obey prepare us and align us to God's time. You have to know who God is in order to be able to trust His timing; let this take root in your mind. *Exodus 34:6-7* *"The Lord, the Lord, the compassionate and gracious God, slow to anger, abounding in love and faithfulness, maintaining love to thousands, and forgiving wickedness, rebellion, and sin...".* God doesn't change; if He has called you to do a thing, He will undoubtedly facilitate it until its manifestation; He is full of integrity; trust him. *"I, the Lord, will make it happen"* when it's God's timing, you don't have to do anything cause the process has prepared you; *THE LORD WILL MAKE IT HAPPEN* when we patient and wait for Gods timing, the goodness of God will happen to you.

I realized that as I was going through challenges, I was praying to God, making my request known to Him according to the Word of God. But I was making the mistake of telling Him what the answer should. Hence when things, in my view, were not happening the way I wanted or at the time I wanted, doubt crept into my head, "Did God hear me, and is He doing something about my request?" Yet, God answered me. It was just the answer I didn't expect or like. This has been a character flaw for many, and we end up questioning the existence and character of God.

Sometimes it felt like the more I prayed about a situation, the worse it got, and when I look at the worldly people, they seem to be getting blessed with everything I have been praying for. *Malachi 3:3-16, "Your words have been harsh against Me," says the Lord, yet you say, "what have we spoken against You?" you have said, "it is useless to serve God, What profit is it that we have kept His ordinance, and that we have walked as mourners before the LORD OF HOSTS? So now we call the proud blessed, for those who do wickedness are raised up. they even tempt God and go free."* I had to repent from harshly speaking to God and not believing in His ability. We have different destinies and running different races, stand on what God has said about you; rest in the fact that He will never change his mind about what he has said. Numbers 23:19 says *God is not a human being, and he will not lie. He is not a human, and He does not change his mind. What He says he will do, He does. What He promises, He makes come true.* God knows what He is doing; allow the process to prepare you for His perfect timing for your breakthrough.

Our challenges, struggles, background, and upbringing play a pivotal role in who we become as adults; it shapes and influences us. You can always take advantage of your background, whether rosey or not, and use it positively to strengthen your character and find your purpose. Though some might need to work more than others and jump more obstacles, victory is possible. Greatness requires sacrifice, hard work, diligence, consistency, patience, resilience, and focus. Whatever season you are in your life right now, favorable or not, do not break your focus on the resolutions and goals you have set yourself. Dr. Tich's words always echo in my ears *"failure is a result of broken focus,"* they re-energize me every time I am discouraged and overwhelmed. As an entrepreneur, the focus will always cause your business to have longevity and grow continuously. The best is yet to come.

Chapter 1

MY CHILDHOOD

I was born and raised in *'kwantuthu ziyathunqa,'* the city of Kings and Queens commonly known as Bulawayo in Zimbabwe. I come from a family of 11 siblings. As a child, I had three stepmothers and two fathers. I was hardly in any stable family set up, but I somehow managed to adapt to any environment that circumstances threw me in. I did yearn for love, though, especially when I stayed with my stepmother soon after my parents divorced.

I started school when I was five years old, and how I got to start school that early is interesting. My mother went with me to my brother's school to pay his school fees one day. While the clerk was attending to her, I was busy reading aloud what was written on the charts and posters in the office. At that moment, we were across the headmaster's office. His office was open, and he could hear me read. The headmaster was impressed, then went to my mom and asked her why she had not enrolled me yet. To cut a long story short, I was registered to start school the following Monday by the time we left the headmaster's office. I was a top student, and I was in the first position four terms in a row. This changed, however, when my parents divorced. As a result, my grades dropped from the top to average and eventually to the bottom of the barrel.

There were several meetings on which each of our parents would take custody of us, and we were consistently asked to pick a side, mum or dad and because we were so tired of the back and forth we ended up with my father and my stepmother after the divorce. There was my half-sister too. It wasn't the best of experiences. My step-sister was allowed to do many things, that I wasn't allowed to do. There were times when I got beaten and when I think about it now, for nothing really. There were times when I wasn't given food, and whenever my father walked into the house from work, I was not allowed to run to him or interact with him. I remember when I tried to get my father's attention that I wasn't getting enough food; my stepmother cooked a big bowl of porridge without sugar and forced me to eat and finish it. I couldn't. I guess you know what happened next. I later developed a eating disorder, I always thought am a foodie, I ate often and the quantities were usually huge. I ate a lot because part of me always thought, I don't know when am going to have my next meal. I have been staying by myself for a long time and I realised that the habit was still there, to unlearn the habit I had to consistently remind myself that the food in the fridge is all mine, it will still be there even later. So, I was constantly in my own corner, careful not to break any rules. I didn't enjoy getting a whooping. I suppose no one has ever really enjoyed getting one.

That was my life until I was in grade 4. When my father and stepmom decided to get a divorce, my father rented my three older brothers and I a place to stay in one of the townships in Bulawayo. We were neighbours with my uncle. It was indeed the most liberated I had ever been. I was happy. I enjoyed living with my brothers, but I don't even think they acknowledged that I was a girl. We played like cats and dogs. However, we lived in a very warm home with love, and I think I felt like a child again for the first time in a while. We didn't have much. We just had a few cooking utensils. We didn't even have a T.V. I was the child who never had stories about what happened on the popular show last night. In a way this protected me from a lot of things, I wasn't negatively exposed to unappropriated media content, But this also made me addicted to TV a lot when I was older, especially when I was now staying by myself, I would spend hours in front of TV, ended up developing insomnia. It was a thing of is it really my TV and I have the right to watch it any time I desired.

My relationship with my father got better. We saw him for a couple of hours during the weekend. We had our uncle and aunt checking on us every day. They made sure we ate, bathed, and went to school.

I got a sense of how it feels like to be in a home filled with com-passion, care, and so much warmth. My uncle was teaching at the school I was going to; he was the MC during our district sports day. I excelled in every race I was running; as he recalls, I filled the whole arena with energy until he couldn't hide that I was his daughter and dropped the mic and ran to the finishing line to congratulate me. My uncle and his family later moved to a bigger house, and my dad looked for a helper to watch over us. She had her moments, but she made sure all our needs were met for the most part. Any time she mistreated me, my brothers stood up for me. Her name was 'Sikhathele,' meaning we are tired.

Once the divorce was finalized, my dad moved with us to a new place. I was the youngest and the only girl, so I got all the spoils and attention. I would sometimes fake being sick so that I could eat something nice instead of the traditional pap and mbhida (green vegetables). Pap and Mbhida is the staple food of every low-income Zimbabwean household, and I'm sure quite a number of Zimbabweans would agree with me that it is not the most delicious meal, especially if you have no choice but to eat it every day.

Life was a bit of a breeze for a while until my father introduced us to his new wife. She was young; she was the same age as my father's firstborn, and of course, she was pretty. Her personality was not too great, though. She was not too accommodating, and we didn't relate very well on many things. A lot of things changed when she moved in with us. My father started to give us less attention. I think it's because my stepmom complained that he loved us more than he loved her. She basically competed with us for our father's attention. I felt this with a huge impact as I was used to having free access to my dad. When I tried to communicate how certain things hurt, it just fell on deaf ears. There was really no platform for me to say anything. My stepmother was not well educated, and that also caused a few issues. We were not allowed to speak English anymore. My stepmom would say we were gossiping about her when speaking English. That also didn't make sense to me, but I could not say anything as a child. She also started keeping food in the bedroom, and we were not allowed to enter the bedroom.

Life became the same as it was before my father divorced my first stepmother. My father didn't do much to defend us. My father used to take us shopping on our birthdays and on my 11th birthday. He asked my stepmother to accompany me to town to buy birthday clothes. I was super excited. However, my excitement was short-lived when we arrived in town and went to every other shop except the clothing store. I returned home without the clothes that I thought I was going to get. I was sad. My father gave me an explanation as to why my stepmother did not buy the clothes for me as per the arrangement. I didn't understand, but there was nothing I could have done about it. That was the last time my father ever attempted to buy me anything.

When my stepmom had a child, I basically became the child's nanny. I would look after the child, feed the child, and wash the nappies. The responsibilities were a lot, and this affected my grades at school. Regular beatings became a permanent part of my life. As a result, I became a very aggressive child. I was consistently fighting at school. I was not able to communicate my feelings. Any conflict with anyone always resulted in a fistfight.

We barely had meals because my step mum kept food in the bedroom. So as much as we would report to my dad, nothing was done.

In grade 7, I moved in with my uncle (my father's young brother) and my aunt; the ones who were our neighbours before my father's second divorce. There was a discussion amongst them, and they decided that would be the best solution for me. I did enjoy living with them. There was a proper family structure. My aunt was somewhat accommodating. I went through to high school living with them. They would buy me some of the stationary, but my father still had to pay for my uniforms and school fees. That was still a challenge for my father. During my first term in high school, I wore home clothes, which got me bullied and laughed at. I could eat three meals a day, so I did not have to worry about where my next meal would come from. I got clothes. My aunt gave me some clothes. However, I still knew at the back of my mind that I was being housed by another family. Therefore, I made sure that I gave them nothing to complain about so they didn't send me back home. I took care of all household chores, followed the rules to the tee; even when I wasn't well, or I had any kind of grievance, I kept to myself so that I was not be a bother to them. I grew up a people pleaser till my early 20s, I immediately took responsibility of the atmosphere of the room, if I entered a room and found every gloomy or sad, I straight away, blamed myself, "what did I do, why are they upset about me and how can I fix it , even though I didn't do anything. I would spend so much time trying to please every-one, at times at the expense of my needs. So went around carrying such a heavy burden. Always the most talkative one in the room, trying to keep everyone's mood happy and no one upset with me .

My grades improved a lot because, staying with teachers encour-aged me to focus on my studies and do better. I was an athlete. I represented my grade house, school, zone, and province. Unfor-tunately, there was never a budget when it came to the nationals. Participating in sports made me feel worthy. It was something I was really good at, and I got a lot of praise for it. Being the school captain for nearly all sporting activities gave me hope of being someone successful in the future. Maurice Green was my favorite athlete, and I saw myself representing my country in the Olympics.

After school, I would come back home as early as I could in order to make sure that food was cooked before the electricity went off. On weekends, I would wake up early and wash everyone's laundry. I did everything that I could to avoid upsetting them. I also wanted them to see my value in their lives so that they could continue ac-commodating me even though I wasn't their biological child.

I would visit my mother during the school holidays and on some weekends. We didn't have a close relationship, though. I did not have a safety net to talk to my mother about anything. Therefore, she didn't know about most of the things that were happening in my life. She didn't know about what was going on in my mind or how I was feeling. She seemed to be dealing with issues of her own. So even when I visited her during school breaks, we didn't talk about anything. I did yearn to be able to talk about certain things that were happening in my life, but there was no platform for me to do that. I didn't know her too well. I was also a child that lived through other people's assistance and sometimes handouts. This somewhat muted my voice because even a family member sexually abused me, and I kept quiet. I did not talk to anyone about it because there was no one I trusted enough to talk to but also because, from time to time, the family member who molested me assisted me with my basic needs.

My brothers and I

On my mother's side its 3 boys and one girl and yes am the one girl and the last one, but technically am the eldest as my mum and brothers say generally because I took the responsibility for the house when I was very little, my nickname at home is "Masisi", meaning the sister of the house. My eldest brother is Lamlela, like any other firstborn he was the deputy parent especially at the era when we stayed by ourselves and dad only came weekends. Extremely talented self-taught mechanic, there is no car he can't fix. He always spoiled me with goodies and protected me from abuse from my stepmoms, both times he was chased away from home was because he was defending me. One thing we didn't get along at, he always called me to bath whilst I was at the climax of street games, I was the captain of the street games like (ma25, mafila ibhodlela, mavika), and like any other child I would refuse to go bath at that time, and he would chase me around the hood, am sure you know by now I was an athlete, most of the times I got away, but the times he got me he would drag me home and made sure I took a thorough bath. Funny thing is he never used to like bathing, as a mechanic he was always greasy and fought with my dad on how he was messing up the blankets. I never liked pap and muroho and when I was up to my schemes pretending to be sick my brother knew what was wrong and he knew what would cheer me up, nkomasi, he always came home with some spoils for me.

Thulani is my second brother and like his name, he was very quiet just like my dad. He was the fashionista of the family, but I have since taken over. Oh, my brother liked keeping clean, smart, and always looking good. I remember at high school he had a skincare routine and used new youth vanishing cream or lemon light, he kept up with the trends. For many reasons, he is my favourite. "don't tell my other brothers", I am sure he doesn't even know. Don't tell my other brothers he is my favourite. I am sure he doesn't even know, for many reasons, he was the comedian among us. Considering our circumstances at that time, he always tried to put a smile on our faces. Do you know those people who find a joke in serious matters! That was him. When we were staying with our first step mum, he used to have a lizard pet and built a small cage for it that stayed in the garden... but well because he we didn't know much about keeping a pet especially like uNtulo it died in a few days, my brother loved it so much we had a burial service for it, the most interesting part was when he was the priest of the service and made us sing *"amagugu alelizwe awosala emathuneni".* He was a great impersonator and consistently showed us what his teacher at school used to do.

Growing up I used to sleepwalk and it was so bad to the extent that though they would hide keys I would find them and try to open the door. When they asked me what I was doing I would say that there was someone calling me outside. My brother volunteered that he would tie me around his waist when going to bed so that I don't go outside. Till today that's one of most thoughtful things he has ever done for me. I was his post girl to his girlfriends; I knew all of them at times I wrote the letters for my brother because my handwriting was pretty good. My brother loved Joe Thomas and made sure I listened to the cassette and replayed it to get the lyrics. This meant that as the post girl I got sweets and some biscuits.

Brunswick, Nqobizitha, is my 3rd brother whom I come after. Growing up we were Tom and Jerry, constantly fighting and arguing. He would try to help me with homework, and I would tell him my teacher didn't say that and refuse his help. After a consultation day at school my teacher indicated that my spoken English was sub-standard, Nqobizitha suggested to my father that we speak English in the house, I have never been so angry with him as I was that day. I always inherited his clothes, so no wonder I was boyish growing up. We had to share everything, I shared a bed with him, and he would say I was breathing too loud. When dad wasn't around, he would bully me so much that I would start crying in the afternoon and it would stop but as soon I knew it was Dad's time to come home I would wait at the gate and resume crying. As a child, I don't know what was satisfying about having my dad scold him.

Growing up he did not like bathing, one evening my dad forced him to go bath, he grudgingly went to bath, and he came out with his Chinese shirt button, buttoned all the way to the neck, when he was asked to take off the shirt, he was completely dry. Nqobizitha liked singing Brenda Fassie songs when he was bathing and always sounded like he was having fun bathing but we later learned he was doing a lot of singing and less of the bathing. On one occasion when we stayed with our helper S'khathele decided to open the door when he was bathing because he always looked dirty even after bathing, only to find my brother fully dressed, his trousers folded to his knees, sitting on the edge of the washing dish splashing water with his feet.

He always had schemes that needed me to take the fall for but knowing dad was very lenient to me I would get away with them. But this changed when he got born again, and he became a Pastor. We are now best of friends, we have a lot of things in common, we love Barcelona, cricket, BMW and Basketball. He has the fondest memories of me when I was younger, and recognized my abilities. He recalls a time when I was 3 years old and I took off and ran to a corner and came back at a speed that 3-year-old could not, he jokes now and says I was racing with the wind. He inspired me to play basketball, and always wanted to train with them, if I failed at anything they did, I would try and try again and they would help me until I achieved.

Everything he did, I did also, he joined a youth arts club and I joined also, we had to dance, act, sing. One day some of the kids who were there saw the way we related and they were shocked that we were siblings playing together and then asked me "you really love your brother, huh, and I said yes. Now my brothers and mum call me mum, this is because at a young age I took the responsibility of the home in all kinds of form like how a mother would. As much as we had our disagreements with Nqo he used to cover for me a lot, I used to lose my school stuff like "skaftin" (lunchbox), jersey, etc and he would give me his and I would lose those too the very same day too, and our helper Skthathele would beat and curse me, he would physically fight her and later she quit, and we were a child-headed family for a while, just me and my brothers.

Chapter 2

BEING BORN AGAIN

When I was in form 2, my life changed forever on the 2nd of September 2005. My history teacher encouraged me to join the scripture union. That's when I learned about the man Jesus, John 6 vs. 35 *"... I am the bread of life. Whoever comes to me will never go hungry, an whoever believe in me will never be thirsty".* Jesus says He is the bread of life obviously isn't about food vs. 33 states for the bread of God is He who comes down from heaven and gives life to the world. I certainly needed the God kind of life. The son of God and part of the Godhead. Most of the time, I felt I was in absolute darkness with no light whatsoever, and I couldn't see anything. I was an angry, bitter, short-tempered, hopeless, dim-witted, aggressive, low self-esteem girl who had difficulty regulating her emotions. I certainly needed the saving power of Christ.

Jesus is telling us in John 8 vs 12 *"When Jesus spoke again to the people, he said, "I am the light of the world. Whoever follows me will never walk in darkness, but will have the light of life.....* that He is the light and can bring anyone out of the darkness. On my first scripture union attendance, I got born again. That was the best time of my life. The scripture union club became a place of solace for me. That's when I felt the desire to know more about God, read the Bible more, and pray more; knowing more about God gave me a fighting spirit, hope, a renewed spirit, and a fresh outlook on life. As much as my circumstances were still the same, I was happier; you wouldn't know if anything wrong or sad was happening to me. It gave me hope that even if my life was not the way I wanted it to be and I didn't have things that I felt I needed at the time, it was definitely going to get better. It gave me hope that everything would go well for me one day.

I grew in spirit, and I began to pray. We were being taught the word of God, understanding the power we possess. I was praying for people. I was praying for the sick. My uncle and my aunt were also prayerful, and they were regular churchgoers. However, I got into trouble with them twice when my other friend and I prayed for people until demonic spirits started manifesting. One fateful day from the scripture union at school, we attended an interdenominational afternoon prayer session and at one of a leader's homes on our way home like we always did. Listen, we were radical anywhere we heard there was prayer we were there, but we did these in secret that our guardians didn't know, we always managed to arrive home on time before they arrived and having done all our household duties. Back to the fateful day, as we left scripture union, we had an excellent service, drunk in the spirit, uniforms dirty because of rolling on the ground, we attended the prayer session. As we were praying, my friend started manifesting legions of demons, seeing dead people, screaming and shouting, and her leaders started laying hands and praying for her. Honestly, at this point, I was praying for her to be delivered already because I was now looking at the time; we could not afford to arrive home late.

Well, she stopped manifesting, and the meeting came to an end, and we rushed home. As we walked home from our conversation, I soon discovered that she was experiencing some abuse at home; she was an orphan staying with relatives. She always complained about her living situation. She started to cry as she was sharing her current situation and attempted to throw herself on oncoming vehicles; by the grace of God, I caught her on time. With what we had since learned, the hope we have in the Lord, I shared with her some scriptures and words of encouragement, and we soon arrived at the place. Unfortunately, as soon as she got to the gate, she fell on the ground and started manifesting again; oh my goodness, was I not terrified?

Not only because of the manifestation as I was still young in the Lord, but how do l explain this to the not-so-believing relatives? It was getting late, what will I tell my uncle, am responsible for supper, what will happen should there be no electricity as usual. Because her guardians went to the same church with the leaders from the prayer session we were coming from (if only I had a cell phone), I ran back to notify them what had just happened, and they assured me that they will go there and attend to her, I then dashed home. At that moment, I could tell the holy spirit was saying something, but I didn't know; all I knew was something was brewing. When I got home, the ambiance was different; my uncle and aunt were not there, my cousin was cooking, this was so unlike him; I nervously changed my uniform and waited, praying for what was brewing.

Moments later, my aunt arrived spitting fire; she dragged me by the ears to my friend's place, who lived about 200m from us. She asked what happened; when I tried explaining, she interrupted, saying, "you going around in every prayer session and insulting demons." Upon arrival at the house, it was packed with leaders from her church, including the pastor, they were still praying, and now she had lost her sight; she claims she could see her dead parents. It was just chaotic. When I entered the room, they were praying for her. She sensed that I was there and shouted my name; I trembled out of fear and confusion. Then, under the pastor's instruction, I began to pray for her; I felt the holy spirit say to me, "You can do it," and guess what? I did; as I prayed for her, the demons left her, and she was free. I was then asked what had happened; I was questioned about the scripture union and prayer session; imagine a room of more than 20 church leaders, including my uncle and aunt, it was nerve-wracking, but I did it anyway.

My guardians looked at me disapprovingly. That night was very, very long; when we got back home, I was stanchly reprimanded, why I have been going around in every prayer meeting, laying hands on the sick, how I have made them enter homes that they didn't know about. Understand my uncle was also still growing in the things of God; they were of the belief that the gifts of God are gradual and there is a process, you get born again, then you go for a lesson on discipleship. You learn about Holy Spirit, then you receive Him, and finally, you start operating in the gifts; while there is some truth in this, it is not complete. So one can get born again, receive the gift of speaking in other tongues, and at the same moment begin to operate in the gifts of the Holy Spirit like what happened to me. They did not fully understand how this fourteen-year-old girl that just got born again was doing all this.

In the days that followed, I tried to stay away from trouble, stopped attending prayer meetings after school, but continued with Scripture Union, which was honestly the highlight of school days. I went to Pumula High School, a well-known notorious school that barely had anything expected good to come from it. My brother Nqobizitha and his friend actually opened the scripture union, and we just grew it as they graduated. From that time, we always prayed for our school to change in every sphere radically, and we started seeing change, our pass rate improved, teenage pregnancy rate dropped, less bullying, less bunking, more students and teachers got born again. I remember a rally for the end of term; there were so many attending that we had to rent a church close by to accommodate everyone. Further followed the other encounter that also got me into trouble after our spirit-filled scripture union meeting. The presence of God was dense, a hair-raising kind of atmosphere; it was so thick you cut it with scissors.

On my way home, I could still feel the presence of God, and diagonally to where I stayed, a friend of mine who attended a different high school but met for combined scripture unions. As I passed her gate, she was busy watering the garden, we shared a greeting, and I waved to her, and she fell down and immediately I knew what's happening. I rapidly went in to help her up and take her inside the house, and she was now praying in other tongues; I prayed with her, but honestly, part of my prayer was, "Lord do your will but don't let your will take too long," don't forget that my uncle had said I must stop these numerous prayer meetings. Well, a few minutes later, it seemed God had answered my prayer, and I left, but the atmosphere was still so charged up with the anointing.

When I got home, I could barely lift a pot and cook or do any house chores, so saturated in the spirit, but I tried my best to contain it. I was sent to get vegetables for supper around the corner and as I was heading there passing my friend's place, I heard noise in the house, things falling and breaking, you can imagine what went through my head "not again, " I actually decided I was not going to engage any further, and I ignored it and continued to fulfil my task. On my way back, the Holy Spirit was nudging me to check on her, so I obeyed and went in; she was on the floor groaning in the Spirit. The furniture was all over the place. You would swear a tornado struck the place. Sat her on the chair, which was a tremendous task, tried to tidy up the place and told her, "girl, you have to try to contain and hold it in" I honestly don't really know what I meant, but I just wanted it to not go any further, my uncle could not hear about this.

I left again because I had the vegetables and I needed to finish preparing supper. Like before, I felt that something was brewing, and I began to pray and prepare myself. The school were my aunt was teaching prompted my aunt to renew her ID, so we had to undo her hair because, in Zimbabwe, you cannot take an ID picture with any hair extensions, so we spent the night unplaiting her braids. Around midnight, there was a knock at the door; everyone was rambling about who it could be at this time of day; my uncle went to the door and attended to it.

They had a brief conversation at the door, and they later invited the person in, and they sat at the dining table, and I was called to the room. I didn't know what to expect, but I knew it had to do with what had happened earlier with my friend. At the table, it was my friend, her drunk dad, step mum, my uncle and aunt; The father was demanding I explain what I did to his daughter because his daughter was shivering. After all, she felt like her bones and joints were breaking, and she had told him what had happened in the afternoon out of fear. She was also frightened of what was happening to her; she had never experienced it before as much as she knew about the Holy and having experienced being slain before.

I later learned he was very strict; that's why we could only play with my friend and always interacted through the fence. He wanted to turn me over to the police, saying I was trespassing, bewitched her daughter, and I needed to pay for the damages done to the furniture. How do I explain the things of the spirit to someone drunk? Where do I even start? I elucidated on how the events unfolded in the afternoon in detail, praying inside according to Matt 10vs 19-20 "but when they hand you over, do not worry about how or what you are to say, for what you are to say will be given you within that "very" hour, for it is not you speaking, but the Spirit of your Father speaking through you. I apologized, and so did my uncle on my behalf; he seemed to calm down and noted I should never be seen near his home or daughter or else I would experience the full extent of his wrath, and all the above charges would be reinstated. As they left my uncle and didn't say much, I was asked to go back to my father's house a couple of days later till the end of term.

I was embarrassed to go to church with them because I didn't have clothes. I only had one decent outfit for church that I wore every Sunday religiously. So, I would let them go first and then follow after.

One Sunday, when we were at church, the pastor announced that someone in the congregation had back pains, and a young person needed to pray for them. I knew I was supposed to pray for that person. I was scared at first, but my confidence in Christ overrode the situation, and I went to the front. I stood in the front, and I could also feel the person's pain in my body. To my surprise, my aunt stood up. I couldn't believe it. However, I gathered courage, and we prayed until she felt better. I was also humbled that my aunt also gathered the courage to come to the front of the church not only for me to pray with her but also for her.

Church was always amazing. It was one of my favorite places to be. I enjoyed going to church with all my heart. It helped me deal with a lot of challenges that I was facing at the time. At school, I didn't have books to write in. I would sometimes use one book for more than two subjects. My school fees were always outstanding, and I would sometimes be sent home. At first, it would be many of us, until I was left by myself.

I always felt the need to overcompensate with the people that looked after me so that they could always accommodate me. I made sure that they were always happy. If they were sad, I always felt it would be because I did something wrong. I always felt compelled to please them so that I was accepted. It was not an easy life, but I am grateful that I got born again at a young age because the ministry and the love of God gave me hope. I knew that there would come a time in life where I would look back and say I made it.

Chapter 3

MENSTRUATION

I got my first period when I was in form 2 as well. Of course, I didn't tell anyone. I mean, who was I going to tell? However, my aunt found out when I accidentally left a stain on the toilet seat. It happens to most of us, especially when we are still starting out and I didn't have pads. So she gave me money to go and buy tissue. I would use tissues when I was on my period, and going to school during those days was the worst. I was overwhelmed. I was sometimes emotional. Above all, I was uncomfortable.

As I grew older, I came to realize that time of the month will always need extra caution and will always be uncomfortable even when you are wearing pads or tampons. Now imagine being in your early teens, experiencing menstrual cycle for the first time, and then having to use tissue, newspapers, or a piece of cloth as a pad. I would be constantly worried about staining my uniform while in class. Sometimes I would wait for everyone to leave the class before I stood up. Tissue is not the most comfortable thing to use as a pad, but that's what I had, and when it was finished, I couldn't ask for more money to buy more tissue. I didn't dare to ask for more.

I would resort to using a newspaper. It was even more uncomfortable. The corners of the newspaper would hurt my inner thighs. I had to be innovative. I figured if I put the newspaper inside a sock, it wouldn't hurt as bad, and the newspaper would stay a little longer without getting wet. I was under performing at school, low self esteem, and timid.

I didn't like what I had to go through whenever I was on my periods when I was still a teenager, and I would not wish that experience on any other young woman regardless of their circumstances. Menstrual health management is one of the big issues in Zimbabwe and Africa at large. About 72% of schoolgirls in rural areas do not use commercial sanitary wear, resorting to unhygienic means, while 62% miss school every month while menstruating.

Women constitute 60% of the illiterate adult population as the school dropout rate is still high, particularly among female students. Many girls drop out of school at the onset of menstruation partly because there are no friendly facilities at most schools. In addition, lack of access to menstrual health management is a barrier to girls' education. This impacts several UNs Global Goals, including Goal 1 to end poverty, Goal 4 for good education, and Goal 5 for gender equality. As a result, girls are being left behind and missing out on their education and employment potential.

The situation in most countries is dire as girls are too poor for menstruation. Some young girls resort to using weeds, leaves, and cow dung instead of sanitary pads, compromising their health in the long run. There is still such a huge stigma and taboo around periods. There is still a great need for menstrual education at homes at schools, as this will break the communication barrier and shade light and possible health issues related to it and safe products to use. It is a very painful experience that disregards the dignity of a woman. Women don't choose to be on their periods. It's a natural process, but those that cannot afford sanitary pads have to feel humiliated every month for something they have no control over. That's why I now run a sanitary pad and toiletry drive for young, disadvantaged women because I know how it feels like not to be able to afford basic needs like sanitary pads. It's self-funded and appeals to individuals and governments to partner and have a significant impact on dealing with this issue.

I was this old when I learnt about PMS (Pre-Menstruation Syndrome) which basically is a group of changes that happen before a woman's monthly period. I would experience constipation no matter how much I tried drinking water, eat vegetables or take a laxative it seemed not to be helping anyhow. When I went to the doctor and he couldn't identify the cause or solution. I did a little research on google and WebMD explains my symptoms. PMS has a vast signs including fatigue, constipation, migraines mood swings, social withdrawal, trouble falling asleep, food cravings, lack of concentration etc. Just imagine experiencing all this as teenager, with no knowledge or control of what you going through, to top it up you have no access to hygienical sanitary wear. I am of the opinion that, there is more the government can do to curb this issue, with condoms being at anyone's disposal in many government facilities, yet one chooses to have sex, while menstruation is a natural process that happens for the rest of their lives involuntarily .

I always wandered do my brothers even know what's happening to me, if they did are they wandering what am using considering our situation at home or they were also dealing with their own issues. May be each one of us leaving with a girl child must be perturbed about during that time of the month what does she use.

I should say that, even in those times when I could not talk to anyone about my needs as a child and a young woman, the love of God kept me.

Chapter 4

LIFE AFTER HIGH SCHOOL

L ife after High school was equally challenging. The challenges were somewhat different, but they were challenges nonetheless. However, before I delve into that experience, I would like to mention that even if I didn't attend most of my A-level classes because I had outstanding school fees, this forced me to drop out of school. I am grateful that my relationship with God had grown stronger; I understood my position in Christ. I consistently reminded myself I am going to make it, That somehow, I will be a success. (sidetrack, I remember when I got born again, been surrounded by young people fired up God, faith like the one to move mountains, we had just learned the power of confession.

Romans 10vs 9, "if you declare with your mouth, Jesus is Lord," and believe in your heart that God raised Him from the dead, you will be saved. The verse states that by confession, we attained our birthright, OUR CONFESSIONS RULE US, serving power comes from confession. *Proverbs 6 vs. 2, "you have been trapped by what you said, ensnared by the words of your mouth.* What we say with our mouths activates the power to create and destroy. The word of continues to bring to light that words created the heavens and the earth. In Genesis 1vs 3 we see the phrase, "and GOD said." So we took up the lesson and confessed, declared, and prophesied into our lives. *Acts 2 vs. 17, "in the last days God says, I will pour out my Spirit on all people, Your sons and daughters will prophesy, your young men will see visions and old men will dream dreams,"* we started giving ourselves names of what we wanted to be when we grow up, I recall Xolani World changer Ncube. I decided to name myself Elinah SUCCESS Mangena. I am sure many may be thinking, is "Success" part of my legal name? Quite a number of people call me that right now.

This led me to believe that whatever I do has to be a success; that's the approach I took when I was preparing for my A-level exams as a dropout. With having to cover half of the syllabus by myself, my reading had to be very strategic and very effective. Also, considering that at my age in most black family home setups, many if not all household chores are your responsibilities, and, mind you, I had taken ARTS, subjects and they demanded a lot of reading. I remember praying a prayer saying Lord, like Daniel may I be wiser and have an excellent spirit. He was wiser than the princes and presidents of his time. The Holy Spirit led me to topics that would come out in, the exams and my memory sharpened in time of need so that I will be able to remember what I read *John 14vs26, "and I will ask the Father, and he will give you another advocate to help you and be with you forever...* Lord, you have said you will instruct me and teach me in the way I should go. You will guide me with your eye, and behold, that's what happened.

I managed to pass with a whopping 11 points. It was a very proud moment for me. I couldn't believe that I had done it. I cannot take full credit, of course. It was all God. He had proven himself again.

Anyway, since I had little to no resources to further my education after high school, I started to look for work so that I can be able to save money and send myself to university. I wanted to study law. I got my first job at 19yrs as a fruit and vegetable merchandiser at a retail supermarket on Herbert Chitepo. It was one of the most reputable retail stores at the time in Bulawayo. The salary was not a lot, but I got a bit of financial independence. I was able to buy myself pads for the first time with my salary. I was able to buy myself brand new clothes every once in a while and help my mother with some household bills. That made me feel great about myself. It motivated me to even work harder.

I was later moved to work in Gwanda in a new shop. This move was gruesome. I was 19 years moving to a small town that I barely knew for this new shop. The company did not sufficiently finance our move. We didn't have accommodation. The day we traveled, we spent the night at some squatter site where most illegal gold miners (makorokoza) stay with no water or electricity. It was not safe at all. I discovered that I have a cousin sister who stayed in the town, and I moved in with them. Gwanda is small. There isn't much to do or room for growth. Remember, I started working so that I could finance my tertiary education. After successfully establishing the fruits and vegetable department in Gwanda, I was recalled to OK Stores along Jason Moyo. It was "the Sandton" of grocery shops by then. My salary was better but barely was I making ends meet considering the work I did and also the inflation rate in Zimbabwe.

There was a point my salary only afforded me a few taxi rides,10kg mealie meal, 2ltrs cooking oil and 3 kgs of beef and some of my toiletries. I don't think one can stay in the Zimbabwean economy and not believe in God because you have to exercise your faith in everything. This is the season I learned the principle of tithing for financial breakthrough. OK, Jason Moyo is located a few streets away from church so, between 12 noon to 1 pm, there was lunch hour service running.

I always made it a point to attend the church service. One afternoon pastor Edgar Moyo was ministering according to Malachi 3vs10, Bring the whole tithe into the storehouse, that there may be food in my house, test me in this, says the Lord and see if I will not throw open the floodgates of heaven and pour out so much blessing that there will not be room enough to store it. Tithing has nothing to do with giving God money; when God sets up a principle, it's not to His benefit to us. It's a management training program. It shows our ability to be accountable, honesty. This is preparation for much to come. Giving the capacity to be able to take managerial or leadership positions.

Building entrepreneurial skills *Luke 16vs10, "whoever can be trusted with very little can also be trusted with much, and whoever is dishonest.* In the book of Malachi 3vs10 it's the only place in the Bible where He gave us the permission to test Him in this principle and see what he would do. You know when God dares, you are guaranteed results. I started practicing this principle, some clients would tip me at times, and I made sure I took 10% of the money and gave it to the Lord, as if immediately I could see the manifestation of the principle, somehow I was able to meet my monthly needs with a salary that was so little. Let's not mistake the fact that God is not a jukebox; all this must be done in faith. I also wanted to apply for my passport and travel to South Africa. It was depicted as the land with greener pastures, after all.

As fate would have it, one of my regular customers would give me tips, and I would save them and tithe. One evening, he came through and gave me a tip for 50usd, which was the exact amount required to apply for the passport. I requested a day off and traveled to Gwanda, and applied for my passport. The day I collected my passport was such a great highlight, one step towards my goal to travel.

On another afternoon, he came through again, complimented my customer service skills, communication skills, and offered me a job in his automotive company in Kwekwe. I didn't think twice; we were on our way to Kwekwe the following day with other girls that he had recruited. I guess I have a thing for starting new things.

I should mention that my first experience of sleeping at a hotel was in Kwekwe, 2011. My first experience of using a fork and knife when having a meal was in Kwekwe. Yes, I ate a lot that day. The food was delicious, and I was at liberty to eat as much as I wanted to. In those moments, I felt lighter, and that I got reminded that my drive-in life would eventually pay off. I worked in Kwekwe for a while. The experience was great, but it became difficult to make money since the country was going through an economic depression, and I knew I had to move on.

That year in August, one of my cousins was getting married, and she had asked me to be one of her bridesmaids. Every weekend I would travel to Bulawayo from Kwekwe for all the bridal team's meetings. The wedding attracted all our family members from all over. Her brother came from South Africa. After the wedding, he hung around a bit, and as he was making plans for him to travel back, I just decided to go back with him. At that point, I didn't know where I was going to stay or what I was going to do; all I knew was I needed change, an opportunity for financial growth, and have an opportunity to further my studies.

Chapter 5

MY FIRST TIME IN JOHANNESBURG

I came to Johannesburg by bus, a chicken bus to specific. It was so uncomfortable. When we left Bulawayo, the bus experienced two breakdowns before arriving in Gwanda, which was 2 hrs away. On the third breakdown, they had to call another bus to take us through. We eventually made it through the border. Immediately the air was fresher. It smelt like hope. The journey wasn't too long because it was my first time traveling to South Africa. I was going to live with my distant uncle, but he was my uncle nonetheless.

Let me tell you a funny story; when I was still back home, we watched a lot of South African content via DSTV. This means we were exposed to the TV adverts, and the most frequent was KFC adverts so, one of the things I had promised myself was that as soon as I touched down in South Africa, I was going to spoil myself with a KFC twister. On our first stop at the South African side, I went straight to KFC and got myself a twister. I thoroughly enjoyed it.

I got off at Park station, and I looked for taxis along Eloff street that were going to take me to Yeoville as I was directed. My first culture shock was boarding a taxi where one of the passengers sitting in front had to count the money and give fellow passengers change and then give the driver the money. You also opened and closed the door for yourself when you got off. I am so glad I didn't sit in front. Where I came from, there were taxi conductors who counted the money and opened the taxi doors. I asked the driver to drop me off at the restaurant that my uncle said I should drop off at. I waited there for a moment, and he came to fetch me.

Everything about Johannesburg was different from Bulawayo. The tall buildings and just how everything was happening so fast. Everyone seemed to be busy with something or rushing somewhere. I was excited, though. I looked forward to eating the food that I sometimes saw advertised on TV. My uncle fetched me and took me to his flat where I was going to be staying with him and his child. It was a tidy flat, and other people had their own households in the same unit. That didn't bother me at all because I was used to sharing space with other people.

In the month of my arrival, I traveled to Durban with my uncle to his permanent place of residence. I got to see the ocean for the first time. It was just surreal. Walking down the beach, and experienced everything that I had seen on TV in my real life. We visited uShaka Marine, and I was extremely scared to walk in my bikini but eventually got over it and had fun.

I got a job about a month after I relocated to Johannesburg. I was working for a betting company. As I was going to the interview, I was quite nervous. I wasn't sure what to expect. I was still trying to adjust to the environment, and it was my first exposure to a business of that nature. I only knew this one thing as long as I went with God. All things work together for my good. It reminded me of what the Word of God says *Deuteronomy 11vs 24 "every place on which the sole of your foot treads shall become yours."* I prayed the same prayer like the one I prayed when I was writing my A levels. In the waiting area, there were returning candidates for the interview and were expressing how tough the last round was, how difficult the questions were. I soon realized the seriousness of this, and slowly, fear started to creep in. I went to the bathroom to gather myself together. It's easy to lose yourself, lose positivity and focus depending on what people say. It's not fun to hang around negative people.

Looking back, I realize the lesson l learned on that day was negative people have negative effects on one's health and success. Scientific research indicates that negativity is contagious; no matter how positive you are, negative people can affect your life unless you take the right precautions. Negative attitudes can also affect your intelligence and ability to think. We will later in the book discuss this topic further. So, I immediately silenced any other voice that wasn't Godly and carried the promises of God. I made sure am carrying my weapon, the sword, the Word of God. *Joshua 2 vs. 2 "... certainly the Lord has given all the land into our hands, for all the inhabitants of the land have melted because of us".* So I got the job in my first interview.

The work environment was quite competitive, and my boss was tough. Some of my colleagues were quite comfortable throwing vulgar words in the workplace. I refused to be called names, and that earned me the name Pastor E. That was very foreign to me because I wasn't used to casually cussing around. I was also shocked when some of my colleagues' addressed women that were old enough to be our mothers with their names. I wasn't used to such behaviors. After all, it was professional nothing is wrong with that. However, I survived and thrived.

I was able to pay rent, buy food and go to downtown Johannesburg and buy some clothes. I frequented Small street a lot. I couldn't believe how affordable things we there considering how much I was earning; my first salary was R3000, which, according to me, was a lot. Let's not forget where I was coming from. I was earning 50usd also R800 a month, and the big reason I was comfortable shopping at Small street was that I was buying from flea markets where I was coming from. That was a big deal for me. As time went on, I got a promotion at work mainly because I knew sports very well and my maths was pretty good, which is what the business required a lot. It was also another defining moment in my life.

My first promotion was to the horse racing department, and it was tough as it was the first time being exposed to the sport. My manager was extremely firm; many times, he made me cry, and I almost quit, but I later became his favorite. After a few months there, I got promoted to a position where I had to work with the owner of the company side by side; I would visit the bathroom several times just to recoup and gather myself and buy some time. There was no room to make a mistake. One single mistake could cost the company millions. It would be impossible to take a break on busy days nearly every day. I had to star at three screens in front of you, watching to see what the competition was offering and making sure we were competitive but not running at a loss. I would watch every client's bet; it certainly did require a lot of mental muscle and ability to work under pressure with different kinds of people from different backgrounds.

I was working throughout the week with only one day off a week, and this barely gave me time for any social life or time to study. I appreciated the salary increase, but it was still difficult to make ends meet because I had registered to study law, so I had to pay my school fees, and I soon discovered that rentals are pretty expensive.

Black Tax; I think every black child can agree with the fact that the moment you start working, you take up your family financial responsibilities; there is usually no room to invest in yourself. This means fewer opportunities to save for the future, reach financial goals such as buying a house and create generational wealth. At first, I really misunderstood this concept, wouldn't anyone who is in a position to help their family do just that? Black Tax exists because of an economically unjust and uneven landscape in African societies. Considering the Zimbabwean economy and knowing that my family needs to make ends meet, without asking, one will feel a need to share what they have with their extended families.

This is largely attributed to our Ubuntu grounding and philosophy. We cannot run away from the fact that some families take advantage and really make sure they suck you dry. They always assume you are in the city of gold and money then grows on trees, or you pick it on the streets. Wisdom is required to have balance in prioritizing. One must be able to consistently invest in themselves; this will later give you a larger capacity to afford to help them without at the same causing you to suffer. I personally had a conversation with my family about my plans and that for a certain period, I can only help them up to a certain level, so I am able to reach my goals. I realized I had to work for almost 5yrs and I had nothing to show for it.

1ˢᵗ Timothy 5vs8 "if anyone fails to provide for his own, and especially for those of his family, he has denied the faith (by disregarding its precepts) and is worse than an unbeliever (who fulfils his obligation in these matters) AMP

Paul consistently wrote to the Saints, how to live life full, every-where the Word of God gives explicit instruction that as a believer we need to provide for our relatives, should we not do this, we compromise our faith, and we are living worse than unbelievers. Remember, when God gives an instruction, the principle is to our benefit. This means when we do this, we will live better lives. We need to joyfully give, without complaint, according to *2 Corinthians 9vs7. "Let each one give (thoughtfully and with purpose) just as he has decided in his heart, not grudgingly or under compulsion, for God loves a cheerful giver (and delights in the one whose heart is in his gift)"* this is the proper mindset you should have when giving. Remember God searches the heart; some give because it makes them look better than 'others in the family and need to be worshipped. Or be regarded as important. Giving connects us and helps to build happier families.

In an age where isolation and loneliness are all too common, giving to one another serves as an important reminder that we are all connected and need to support each other. Am sure after the Covid pandemic, we can agree on that. And when refer to giving it's not referring to mammon, but also of your time, ideas, links to opportunities, etc. Honestly, when was the last time you visited some of your relatives, spoke to them on the phone just to check their wellbeing. As Christian, we are quick to do this for strangers or our church family (not that there is anything wrong with that) and forget that charity begins at home. When I had the conversation with some friends, one said, 'but these relatives don't check on me or were never there when I needed help' etc., but what's your God assignment? We are instruments used by God to minister to His people. Don't you want to rewrite some of these unkind family dynamics? Break the cycles of strife and hatred? When one is born again, they are a new creature's old things have passed away, and all things have become new. I am not saying it's easy, and certainly, you cannot do it by yourself; you need the help of the Holy Spirit.

Are you looking to enter a season of greatness? And you are asking yourself how? *Proverbs 18vs16 "a gift opens the way and ushers the giver into the presence of the great"*... giving comes with a presence, environment, and ambiance. The Word of God gives us tools on how to be GREAT AND MEET UP THE GREAT. If you are feeling drained, weary, enervate, effete, maybe you need to check your giving habits. *Proverbs 11vs25 a generous person will Prosper.* WILL, there are no two ways about it. The word refreshed may be hinting at the feeling of joy and contentment one experiences when being charitable. There are two areas of the brain that become more active when a person gives. The first is the mesolimbic pathway, the same area that distributes the feel-good dopamine chemicals associated with money and food. And secondly is the subgenual area of the brain, which plays a key role in formulating social attachment. After all, maybe money can buy happiness when you give it away.

Here are some Scriptures that might help develop a giver's character.
- *Psalm 37vs21*
- *Matt 6vs3-42*
- *Proverbs 3 vs27*
- *1 Chronicles 29vs14*
- *Luke 6vs38*

Chapter 6

NAVIGATING LIFE

Growing up, I was always a tomboy. I mean, I lived with my three brothers and my father for the most part of my upbringing. I was barely exposed to the girly stuff. The only skincare routine I knew was the sunlight green bar soap and Vaseline blue seal. I was so clueless that in my attempt to fit in, everyone in Johannesburg looked like they were bathing with milk and water. Zizo Beda was the ambassador for Garnier, and she was advertising the Garnier toner, and of course, she looked stunning, and I so wanted to look like her. I went on to purchase the toner, but hey, the ad didn't show when she was using the face wash toner then moisturizer. So, I continued with the normal routine "according to me" but added a new step. SUNLIGHT GREEN BAR SOAP – VASELINE – GARNIER TONER and I would head out for work.

I couldn't understand why my skin was so dry after the toner, and there wasn't so much accessibility of internet as now, and there was no one around to tell me otherwise. If you like me then and you don't know what the toner is for, it removes any last traces of dirt, grime, and impurities stuck in your pores after you wash your face. Toner also balances your Ph levels, smoothes skin by refining rough patches, and improves skin tone. It comes in a water-based liquid form, and you need to apply a moisturizer after applying it.

However, when I moved in with my roommate, Novuyo, things changed. Actually, life became great. We lived in a big bachelor's flat with a separate kitchen. I would say it was my first interaction of what life should be like. I was introduced to what would have been my own version of a soft life back then. I was introduced to face washes, makeup, buying clothes at affordable shops in malls, weaves, learning new recipes. Basically, she was my guardian angel; she always did my makeup, going to church on Sundays, and other church activities. She forcibly asked me to buy my first Brazilian, her words "You are buying this hair, if you don't have money, you will pay for it in installments," she took me to Edgar's to buy my first lipstick in 2014, and I got my makeup done. It felt like a bother then, but I am glad God gave me someone like her in that season. My roommate always insisted that I wore makeup and invested more in my appearance.

I was the CEO of the color-blocking trend. I was happy. My roommate was very girly, and she gradually rubbed it off on me. I also got to date a little bit. I enjoyed staying with her, and life was fun. I cannot talk about her not mentioning our love for Pap, muroho, and vegetables. We basically could have it any time of the day. Also, don't forget that I grew up with boys, so Novuyo was more than a roommate and col-league. She was/is my sister. After 3yr years of staying together, she had to move in with her husband. I realized how much I learned from her; my love for makeup was clear. So, I endeavored to try it myself, and she always said you must always use a brown eyebrow pencil. So, I went to Small Street, got myself one and got my first foundation by myself, and started emulating what she used to do.

I resigned from the betting company because it didn't give me much room to study. I got a job as Telemarketer. I appreciated the working hours, holidays, weekends lunch hour, but it was also strenuous. It was emotionally draining; we all know how we feel about receiving calls from telemarketers, the phone consistently being dropped on you, hearing hundreds of Nos. There are psychological effects of being told no; it all feels like rejection. Rejection can influence emotion, cognition, and even physical health. Imagine this, struggling to make even one sale the whole day and sitting next to someone who literally seemed to make a sale every call they make. My performance was fairly average. That place made a prayer warrior out of me. There were some black magic items you would find on people's desks to help them get sales. Or they would have illicit relationships with managers to ensure that they would get quality leads, extra sales, and more lucrative campaigns. At that point, I had no backup plan. The salary was commission-based, so my income was unstable, but I stayed there because I had to take care of all my financial obligations. The owner of the apartment we were staying in for the last four years decided to sell it, and we had to move out, and the campaign I was working on got cancelled.

So basically, no place to stay, no work. It felt like everything was crumbling down. I moved to a room in Lombardy east and pawned my TV to pay rent and deposit. I started looking for work. The only highlight by then was attending church on Sunday. I needed to believe that I could still be a success at that time. Also, at that time, I lost many friends who were calling me by all kinds of names just because I lost my Job; my financial responsibilities also did not stop.

Fortunately, a friend from church told me about an open vacancy at her workplace. I applied, went for an interview, and got the job. I worked there for a while until they couldn't retain me as an employee because of my immigrant status. My immigration status caused them to underpay me regardless of the responsibilities I held in the office. And the friend that informed me about the Job made sure that

I didn't forget that, at any point of promotion from my bosses, she felt like it threatened her position. The office politics was extremely overwhelming. I managed to keep a level head as much as it was not easy. I had to use a lot of what will Jesus do moments.

The truth is no one wins when it comes to office politics, especially if you are one who tries to get even. Many times, I tried getting even, and it backfired. I learned that I would lose out if you didn't know to handle things well in the office. I asked myself, "What do you do then?" 90% of the time I'm in the office, I cannot afford to spend it in misery, already the salary was depressing? To get answers, I went to my manual to life.

ROMANS 12VS 17-21 ESV Repay no one evil for evil but give thought to do what is honorable in the sight of all. 18 If possible, so far as it depends on you, live peaceably with all. 19 Beloved, never avenge yourselves, but leave it to the wrath of God, for it is written, "Vengeance is mine, I will repay, says the Lord." 20 To the contrary, "if your enemy is hungry, feed him; if he is thirsty, give him something to drink; for by so doing you will heap up burning coals on his head."21 Do not be overcome by evil, but overcome evil with good.

Imagine God saying, let me fight for you, and He is Jehovah El Gibor, the Lord of angel armies.

1st Peter 5 vs 8 Be alert and of sober mind. Your enemy, the devil prowls around like a roaring lion looking for someone to devour. 9 Resist him, standing firm in the faith, because you know that the family of believers throughout the world is undergoing the same kind of sufferings.

Remember who's the real enemy; he would use any possible tool to get to you.

> *Ephesians 4 vs 29 "Let no corrupting talk come out of your mouths, but only such as is good for building up, as fits the occasion, that it may give grace to those who hear."*

Do not engage in the office gossip, backstabbing, sabotage, and foot-dragging. Put yourself in another person's place, and you will understand how it feels to be talked bad about; we need to make a conscious decision to live differently from others. We have to control what we say; it plays a big role in how the world views us.

> *James 5 vs 9 "Do not grumble against one another, brothers and sisters, or you will be judged..."*

We must understand that we all have weaknesses; some people are the way they are because of what happened or what's happening to them. It's not our position to judge cause if someone puts it under a microscope, we would be found faulty. The challenge is not to get negative while asking others to take corrective action.

> *Mark 12 vs 31 "...Love your neighbor as you love yourself..."*

How you treat others is a reflection of how you feel about yourself, it might be that you don't love yourself.

> *Matt 5 vs. 38 -39 "...but I teel you, do not resist an evil person, if anyone slaps you on the right cheek, turn to them the other cheek also..."*

My stepfather always used the African proverb in any relationship ku-lomvundla losithutha. There are times when your best bet at winning would be to let others think that they are ahead of you. I have learned that being underdog has always been my strength. Let them speak ill about you, love them, and neutralize their actions with kindness.

Matt 5 vs 9 "... blessed are the peacemakers for they will be called children of God."

We are Kingdom ambassadors; we look like God, and we need to act like Him. He is Jehovah Shalom, God of Peace. Instead of fanning up strife, we strive for peace and reconciliation.

Philippians 2 vs 3-4 "... do nothing out of selfish ambition, or vain conceit. Rather, in humility, value others above yourselves, not looking at your own interest but each of you to the interests of the others."

Let's not think highly about ourselves, let all pride and selfish desire die and keep others in mind, listen to them and make people feel they are heard rather than argued with.

Gal 6 vs 1 "...Brothers and sisters, is someone is caught in a sin, you who live by the Spirit should restore that person gently...."

We have to learn to be our brother's keeper; we all at some point need some direction, admonishing, and advice. We need to be patient with one another and offer the same to others and restore them gently, not in a prideful way as if you are without any fault of your own.

*Colossians 3 vs 12-14 Therefore, as God's chosen people,
holy and dearly loved, clothe yourselves with compas-
sion, kindness, humility, gentleness and patience. [13] Bear
with each other and forgive one another if any of you
has a grievance against someone. Forgive as the Lord
forgave you. [14] And over all these virtues put on love,
which binds them all together in perfect unity.*

Life became challenging again. I was hopping from house to house without a permanent place to stay. At one point, I stayed with a friend. I then stayed with a brother from church. Sometimes I would visit people for at least two days as the building allowed people to visit for a certain period, and this was so that I could have a place to sleep. I then shared an apartment with a university student, managed to pay the first month but could afford the next rent. We were locked out of the apartment only with clothes on our backs. She went to her family. I was lost on who to go. As we were sharing bills, this affected her greatly, and the lease was in her name. She went to the police station, reported; I was summoned and ordered to pay the rent in 2 weeks. I was terrified and panic striken, I would get arrested if I don't raise up the money within 2 weeks. There was a particular incident when I visited my fellow church friend for the night; she later went around saying I finished electricity without any mention to me. Have you ever heard of those friends you don't want to leave when going to the bathroom, not because you will miss them so much but because you know they will start talking about you when you leave?

*Proverbs 16 vs 28 "A perverse person stirs up conflict,
and a gossip separates close friends .."*

Great lessons about true friendship. Sometimes we are friends with people who have a hidden agenda and don't have friendship qualities. With the people that you consistently associate with, how do you feel when you with them? Do they make you insecure, are you trying to fit in, what role do you play in the group or relationship, what purpose are they serving? Sometimes we call people friends who are not our friends, either just people we know, acquaintances, and colleagues. A true friend is someone who stands up for you; they do everything they can to make sure you stay safe. If they can help, they will do it without reservations or reward. They never repeatedly negatively impact you by spreading rumors. They make it clear where they stand in your life by action and words. They actively act when someone is tearing you down. They are able to be honest about your action, give you perspective, and are full of empathy. You are also not scared to fall in front of them cause you can be authentic around them.

Proverbs 18 vs 24 "...One who has unreliable friends soon comes to ruin..."

One who has unreliable friends soon comes to ruin, but there is a friend who sticks closer than a brother. Evaluate the friends you have and what kind of friend you are, lest either of you is ruined. Let's look at Job and his friends Job 42 vs 10 "When Job prayed for his friends, the Lord restored his fortunes, giving him twice as before." When Job prayed for his friends, the Lord restored his fortunes, giving him twice as before. Are you praying for your friends? Are your friends praying for you? I am glad about the friends that God blessed me with now; I can confidently rely on them. But I had to go through terrible friendships that almost ruined me. By praying for your friends, God can multiply your fortunes. If your friends don't pray for you or support you, it might be that they are envious and they don't want you to succeed, especially if they think they are ahead of you; they will always want you under them.

Scriptures to help you become a better friend and evaluate the friends you currently have and how you can improve your current relationship.
Proverbs 27 vs. 9
Psalms 133 vs. 1
1 Thessalonians 5 vs. 11
Romans 12 vs. 10
Colossians 3 vs. 13
Proverbs 17 vs. 9
Ecclesiastes 4 vs. 10
Job 6 vs. 14
Proverbs 27 vs. 10
Proverbs 22 vs. 24-25

At one point, I didn't know who to go to, and I slept at Park Station. Life was hard, but I couldn't even tell my family back home. They actually expected me to be sending them money as usual. I approached my then YAF (Young Adults Fellowship) leader James "Jimbo" told them about the situation. One of his friends "Bravo," who had left church years back, offered to house me until I found a job. It was a difficult decision to make; how would we navigate staying together considering he was a guy?. But at this point, I was very desperate; any place was better than Park Station, and secondly, I was truly humbled by his offer to help, so I moved in. My stay with him was pleasant; he always made sure there was food in the house and helped me search for employment. I kept on doing everything in my power to look for a job and get back on my feet, and I finally got a job.

I ended up living with my pastor; soon after that, I got a job as a sales consultant. I was able to pay the outstanding rent balance before the date the police order was due. I was really skeptical about moving in with my pastor as much as I didn't know what to expect, it was a moment for rebuilding and restoration. They provided a sanctuary of, hope. They offered me free housing, free food and free life coaching. It was awesome to have people looking out for you and wanting or expecting nothing in return.

As a sales consultant, I had to travel to different provinces of South Africa, selling a trading package. This gave me exposure to different kinds of cultures, backgrounds, and industries. Meeting different people every day was quite exciting and is helping me with my current work. Basically, it was a trading platform that one would use to trade, and we offered training. On my first week after training, l had four deals that week which was a huge deal because each deal was R6000 commission even though one had to cover their traveling, accommodation expenses. This was the first time having such an amount in my account. I managed to clear my debts, and Things got better.

After a while, I met up for the first time with my uncle from my stepdad's side. My stepdad gave him my details for him to contact me and check on me, which he did. He expressed great concern about my well-being, my future plans, and what I needed help with. Unfortunately, on our next meet up he was not feeling well. He had been diagnosed with stage 4 cancer also that time. I met his wife and five kids and the youngest being 2years. It was tough to see him in that state, The strain it was putting on the family emotionally and financially. He passed away a few weeks later. I moved in with my uncle's family upon request from my aunt, and also I realized the need. The family had literally left her by herself soon after the burial, and where I come from, I had learned that after one loses a partner, the aunties and grannies should stay with her for at least two weeks to help adjust, comfort her and help her with the cleaning, kids, etc. Since no one stayed behind, I did. Because I could see that she was hurting and grieving, I took it upon myself to minister to her. I took her to my church, where she got born again, and we consistently read the Word of God.

My aunt at that time was working at a casino for the last eight years, and it required her to work also night shifts; this was now proving difficult to do with a 2-year-old who the husband used to mind while she was doing the night shift. She resigned and took another job that was more flexible. She got a job as a sales consultant at an insurance company. With my field experience, I was able to help her. She would go for training, and I would read the material when she came back. And I took a break from my work to help her in the field as this was her first time doing such a job that required her to pitch and sell a product, have a knack for closing deals, and be self-assured.

I would get to clients and pitch and she would fill the details and do all the required legal confirmation. I wasn't earning a salary, I lived on savings for a while and thought after a couple of weeks I can go back to work.

Chapter 7

THE FIRST STEP TOWARDS THE GREATER CALLING

When I went back to work, I was slowly losing interest in the job, mostly because it required a little bit of lying on our sales pitch, it was honestly uncomfortable. Let me paint you a scenario, basically we were selling a way one can make millions and create a fortune for oneself. Our clientele was basically anyone who wasn't blacklisted. So meeting them up we needed to project the profit we were making money from trading. We had bought a few expensive clothes from factories, wore an expensive perfume, if you didn't have a car, you would just buy a car key to carry around. I didn't have a car so used to use a lot of uber black. If I had to travel somewhere far I would catch a taxi and drop off a few kilometres from my destination and request an uber black and remember the driver is required to open and close the door for me, this made it seem like he was my private driver and used on a pitch at times. At times my car was on service. Because I was trying to save, I couldn't afford to buy expensive perfumes, so I would at times pass at an Edgars perfume station to test some fragrances and leave without buying. The elderly would confirm the contract to purchase the trading software, but you could tell they didn't fully understand but you would just go ahead with the deal to make the sale, knowing that it would be difficult for them to learn and make money as promised. It made me think of my parents signing credit of R26000 using their pension money, I couldn't stomach it, so I started looking for another job.

One afternoon, I had an appointment with a potential client at work. When I got to the client's place of work, they were in a meeting that was to end in an hour. I patiently waited for them in the reception area. While I was waiting, I began chatting with the security lady that was on duty. She complemented the way I had drawn my eyebrows and then went on to request that I draw her eyebrows as well. I casually agreed. Not only did I do her eyebrows but her whole face. The results were impressive considering this was the first time doing a full face beat. She was very pleased. I didn't think it was big deal. Soon after that, my potential client came. She asked the security guard who did her makeup and she pointed at me. The next question from my potential client was, 'how much do you charge?' I got the grip of the conversation very quick and pretended that being a Makeup artist was actually my side hustle. I thought to myself so what I just did has monetary value, and I could have been paid, WHAT!! She informed that her friend was getting married, and they are in need of a makeup artist. She asked me if they can book me and what are my rates, because I was completely clueless about the industry, I insisted I send her a quotation as soon as I got home, this was to buy me time to research on bridal rates etc.

The wedding was meant to be in 3 months and two weeks after the first encounter, the bride requested for a bridal trial, I wasn't aware what they were referring to, we thank God for brother google. They just needed a trail of the look prior to wedding. I had not worked as a makeup artist before. I did not have any tools or resources to be a professional makeup artist. I remember shaking and silently praying in the taxi that the bride had the same complexion as me because the only foundation that I had was the one that I was using for myself when I went to do the makeup trial. I got there you would swear I had a PhD in makeup artist, the only thing I had was my confidence, As much as I didn't have much products, I made sure they believed that I can produce results, but in my head I was extremely worried. She was a shade lighter than me. I did her face, and she was extremely happy and I was puzzled. She told me that she had 9 bridesmaids and how much did I charge!!! I didn't know if it's the same rate as the bride, I just informed her I will send her a quote.

That meant I had 9 more faces to work on where was I to get makeup products for 10 faces, is it even possible to do 10 faces for the same event !! but as always I believed if God can't let me go through something I can't handle, it means I had capacity. I did extensive research on Makeup artistry. I watched videos on YouTube on how to professionally do face beats. I then went to a friend of mine Ayanda Dube who was studying directing and filming to borrow makeup as one of the modules where makeup artistry and her school had provided her with a whole entire professional kit, and I was ready for my Bride and her bridesmaids , well not all ready because I had little to no knowledge of the contents of the makeup kit. Everything I was using I was figuring out its purpose while doing their makeup.

In conclusion, my first booking was a two-day wedding in Drankensberg where I did make up for the bride and her 9 bridesmaids, travel and accommodation paid for. The client was happy with my work. I had no professional background in makeup artistry but I pulled it off and guess what, I made ¾ of my monthly earnings on one weekend, and most of all it honestly didn't feel like work but more also a gateway. I knew I was on to something. That's how the journey started, and I never looked back from then.

I hadn't really thought what this could be and where it was heading to or taking it fulltime. Now and again I would get complimented with my makeup on the Gautrain, taxi and every time it puzzled me and I didn't realize at what level my skill was at. My next bride was also by accident. My cousin needed help with a wedding bridal party steps practice and upon arrival the bride was impressed with my make-up and asked me if I could her makeup on her wedding day. She had some skin issues that at first, I didn't know I would handle them, but was ready to take-up the challenge. What I had to do is I took her to Edgars because she wanted to buy her own foundation, and I knew at Edgars if you buy any makeup products, they do skin assessment and do your makeup. As they were doing skin assessment and how they covered the blemishes, I was taking notes on what I would do on the big day. On her wedding day I was able to deliver and she was par-ticularly impressed and referred a lot of members from her church.. At first, I thought this was going to be a weekend thing or a seasonal thing so I would be able to do it while I do my 8 – 5 job, but soon realised the demand as I started receiving bookings for during the week. I always found an excuse for missing work but it got to a point where I ran out of excuses. I remember having a conversation with God as I contemplated if I should resign and take up makeup artistry full time considering that at that time, I wasn't making any profit yet, any money coming was to buy products. Many people around me dis-couragingly said, the industry is so saturated you not going to make it. You have zero experience how would you penetrate the industry? You don't have enough clients how are you to make ends meet? 'Lord am quitting my job may I get to point where am fully booked' I prayed…. Isaiah 54 vs 4 "do not be afraid you will not be put to shame, do not fear disgrace, you will not be humiliated…" I got the assurance I need-ed and quit my job.

Chapter 8

MY FIRST CELEBRITY CLIENT

A s time went on, I invested in my craft as a makeup artist. I bought more products and did more research in the field of makeup artistry. This made me deliver excellent services to my clients but what also helped me was my ability to confidently walk into a room and seem like I am 100% sure of what I am doing. I never showed any sign of uncertainty or self-doubt. I believe that made my clients trust me even more.

One day I was going for choir practice at church. Something in me told me to carry my makeup kit, and I did. As fate would have it, my sister Ancillary who has been my makeup guinea pig for the longest time, called me and told me that 'Chi' needs a makeup artist urgently, and it didn't register who she was referring to. During those times, I never said no to a booking. I was in a taxi to the client's location in the few minutes that followed. When I got there, the client was one of the ladies that was starring in a popular South African soapie at the time. As usual, I wore my big girl pants and rose to the challenge. I must admit, though, that internally I was nervous; over the years, this person has had her makeup done by the best professionals; I was praying that I was doing the right thing, and I couldn't wait to finish. I sighed in relief when she looked at herself in the mirror and smiled in satisfaction. The work of my hands had yet again shown up for me.

A few days later, I got a call from the same client. She needed my services for her sister's graduation. I was thrilled; I thought she really liked what I did last time. I went there with confidence and delivered to the best of my ability, and when all was said and done, everyone was happy. Every time I could, I had the opportunity to work with celebrity clients or photographers. It always forced me to go do my research practice and execute what was expected as they have had experience with professional makeup artists with incredible skill and experience.

I started getting booked constantly, and I began to work with astounding photographers like Optimass Art, Tendydiz, Inyathi Photography, and SbuDrumlot on different shoots. My sister always referred me to her clients and colleagues; from the beginning, she always sold me as the "baddest" makeup artist in town; this pushed me to improve and get better as I wouldn't want to let her down. Referrals are very important to me; it's such a great honor. It means someone trusts me and my skill so much that they are willing to put their name on the line for my sake. So I always worked hard to impress by doing more than was expected, to honor the person who referred me, and to please the new client. Referrals are a vital tool in growing your business and establishing your brand name as an entrepreneur. Referrals produce referrals; referred clients are loyal. I then ventured into styling as well. On set, I always made sure the client looked impeccable from head to toe, prior to shoot, not that it was my responsibility or am getting paid for it, I always believed that my work shined more if the whole look is aligned, the hair, outfit, nails and how they posed (getting the right angles is important). One of the things that enabled me to grow as a Makeup artist is that the people that I met and worked with within this field believed in me. Most of my bookings came from referrals, which boosted my confidence because it meant my clients loved my work. Most photographers added my services on their packages, until today I still work with them. I continued to invest more in my craft, and I eventually quit my job and worked as a full-time makeup artist.

My first celebrity client became my regular client, and as the blessings continued to shower, I garnered more celebrity clients.

Chapter 9

THE BUSINESS OF MAKEUP ARTISTRY

I managed to find my own place when I gained some financial independence. There were days when I got a lot of bookings and made money. However, there were also days when bookings came in slower, and I didn't know how I would make my rent, but I knew appetite was an incentive to work. I remained invested in my business. The nature of my business also came with some form of backlash. I got backlash from the church because I was wearing what was perceived as a lot of makeup. Red lipstick was also associated with a certain level of indecency. I had to stop going to church for a couple of months; at that point, every Sunday felt like an attack on me. I had to learn how to hear God myself; I was questioning what I was doing and who I was,

IS THERE SOMETHING REALLY WRONG WITH WEARING MAKEUP?

The Bible does not in detail expound on this subject in detail but does not condemn the wearing of makeup but reminds us what's more important is what's inside, your character, personality, and attitude. It's interesting that you find a woman in the Bible wearing makeup, 2nd Kings 9vs30 *".....she put on her eye makeup ,arranged her hair...."* Yes the Biblewarns us that our adorning shouldn't be external 1st Peter 3 vs. 3-4 *"your beauty should not come from outward adornment , such as elaborate hairstyles and the wearing of gold jewelry or fine clothes".* I don't generally fit into the typical girl cause I am opinionated, love dressing up, doing makeup, getting my hair done, fitness, etc. It's as if you can't look good and love God at the same time. Not quite as expected, I tried a lot to fit into the church system and yearned for approval. The more I tried, the more I failed, and this affected my confidence a lot. Someone once said, before you diagnose yourself with depression, check your environment; it must just be the negative people around you.

The majority of women do not like makeup for many reasons. These are some of them.
- Bad experience (I think we all can agree no one likes makeup that is not done well, and everything must be done in modesty and with appropriate motives)
- Its so much work and its time consuming (I think if you enjoy it much , that time is more investment since you know the rewards of putting it on and when you get the hang of it, it doesn't take that long)
- Its expensive (makeup products are quite expensive and you have never have enough products, There is though alternative drug store quality makeup products that can produce flawless work
- They don't know how to apply makeup (one can learn by practicing or getting a professional teach them)
- The mass of men don't like it.. (with the aim at dating and getting married, some men don't consider applying makeup wifely)
- Can cause premature aging/skin problems (but if you exercise a good skin care routine and quality products one will not experience any skin problems.

All the above is subjective dependeding on personal experience and preference. Just because you prefer not to engage in an activity that is not beneficial to you, don't despise it. Remember makeup is an enhancement of your beauty, its like how we do our hair differently, new clothes, its to present us finer..

I learned to take criticism as a point of growth in my life; I realized that life doesn't always introduce you to people you want to meet. Sometimes life puts you in touch with people you need to meet that will help you. They help you by hurting you, to leave you, and breaking your heart. They will also love you, encourage you, and gradually strengthen you into the person you were meant to become. I remained focused on my business, but it affected my relationship with God because I stopped going to church. This was a blessing I learned how to look for God myself; if the very same God my pastor believes and preaches about is the same God I worship, I should also be able to hear from Him

BEING BORN AGAIN!!! AGAIN

I was on the road to self-discovery; the first step was to sit down with myself and ask myself these questions: Who am I am? what is it that I don't like about myself? What do I enjoy most? What and who makes me question who I am and my position? What areas of weakness do I need to work on in my life? What does it mean to be born again? What is my purpose? I evaluated every criticism and started working on my character and personality. There are many things I had to learn and unlearn. This is a hard conversation to have with yourself but very necessary for any individual. This played a major role in my business and how I positioned myself. Being a creative person, a lot of focus has to be invested in what I do. I have to ensure that the skill levels are at their best in order to make the business work. I am not okay inside it will affect the quality of the work too.

John 3 vs. 3-5

Being Born again means a spiritual rebirth, my soul realizes I am a sinner that needs saving Romans 3 vs. 23, and through Jesus, I have the blessing of salvation. Being born again is having a change or transformation of the soul and heart by the work of God's spirit. One spirit consists of three things, the mind (or its disposition), emotions (feelings), and our will (what we determine).

So I had to learn that being born again is a complete process not only in my spiritual state but thoughts and feelings, and these are not instantly done by me confessing Jesus as my Lord and personal savior. It's an ongoing process.

Mind
Romans 12vs 2 "do not conform to the pattern of this world, but be transformed by the renewing of your mind...."

1 Cor 2vs 16

What are the patterns of the world that I mustn't conform to? First, I required a relationship with God of love and not of convenience. Second, I was spending time in the word to know the heart of the father. The more I did this, the more I realized how much I needed to work on myself. Here is one thing I also learned, the more time you spend with God, you feel a lot of sense of unworthiness because God is light, and nothing dark resides in him. So the light exposes any kind of sin or area we need to work in ourselves.

Emotions.
It is an area that holds a lot of control in our lives, this area I am still working on. We are not to let our emotions control our behavior.

Eph 4 vs. 29 "..do not let any unwholesome talk come out of your mouths..."

The sins that God hates most have a lot to do with our emotions, attitude and personality, we tend to neglect this area. (PRIDE, ENVY, LYING WRATH, GLUTTONY, LUST, SLOTHFULNES, and GREED) Without the ability to exercise self-control in any area, we cannot discover who we are, and when abundance comes, we cannot contain it. We always consider what's sinful as, drinking, clubbing, wearing short stuff, smoking, etc.. but Proverbs 6 vs. 16-19, Gal 5 vs. 19-21 shows what matters the most.. It's always good to identify for yourself an area of weakness you need to work on before someone tells you least you retaliate. If I were going to work with different people, with different personalities each day, I would need to have them worked on.

How I discovered my purpose, purpose according to the Oxford dictionary means the reason for which something is done or created or which something exists, So in other words, with the qualities, I have what do I have to offer. What makes your life meaningful. Research shows that people who have found their purpose have a good sense of control, have positive health outcomes, and tend to live longer.

Signs that you're not living in your purpose.
- You're not waking up excited in the morning
- You rarely have high highs
- Your life isn't entirely fulfilling
- You are surrounded by people who are constantly bringing you down
- If you don't have a group in your life whose qualities you admire, that's probably a sign that you're off purpose.

- You are ignoring your dreams because you're scared to move on
- Working a job that depletes your energy
- You feel stuck, and you don't know the next step.

Steps to finding your purpose

Listen to feedback.

It can be hard to recognize the things you feel passionate about sometimes. You are probably displaying your passion and purpose to those around you without even realizing it. Reach out to people and ask them what reminds them of you, what do they think of when you enter their minds. Pay attention when someone pays you a compliment or makes an observation about you. Document these. It will help to zero down your purpose.

Who are you spending time with?

You need to focus on relationships and personal growth. What do you have in common with the right people you hang with, do not only look at those you are obligated to spend time with like, family, colleagues, or fellow students, but also those in your spare time you chose to be with. As the saying goes, you are the company you keep. It's hard to be purposeful and positive when you are surrounded by people who aren't interested in making positive contributions.

Pay attention to who you are with when you feel your best.

Explore your interests

The things you like talking about and the things you enjoy sharing on social media may reveal the things that give you purpose in life. Conversations that move you and you enjoy holding. I always commented on how some artists looked like from their makeup to outfit and hair, and hoped I had the opportunity to help them with styling. I am so glad that I actually had a chance to work with some of them. Give yourself permission to explore, and don't ignore intuition. This will help you to grow to your purpose as well.

Discover what you Love.
This can be a hobby, an activity; consider what type of skills, talents, and passions you bring to the table. Then brainstorm how you might turn your passion into something meaningful to you. Do what you love that pays you as well. Combine your strengths with your passions. In all this, you need some wisdom and revelation. The God factor is very important in making life and career choices. Be patient with the process.

In all this, you need the kindness of wisdom and revelation. The God factor is very important to my life and my career. If you are not born again, it means you are spiritually dead.. "to be carnally minded is death, but to be spiritually minded is life and peace.

Bookings came through, and one of my highlights was flying for the first time to Zimbabwe for a wedding. The wedding was featured on a popular TV show that celebrates weddings, and this resulted in my first TV appearance. Newspaper articles followed soon afterward; the brand Elinah Mangena (esmangena) began to grow. I became noticed as a Professional Makeup artist.

I then hosted my first master class in Zimbabwe at Bulawayo Art Gallery, and the turnout was more than what I expected. Quite frankly, I didn't know what I was doing, but I took a leap of faith and organized a venue with no budget or barely any sponsorship. I am grateful for having great friends who offered all kinds of support they could, advertised the event, and it paid off. It gave me an opportunity to frame out the necessary knowledge I needed. The next masterclass was in South Africa, and it also went well. Women appreciated my work, and some women requested that I teach them some of my makeup skills.

I remember buying a fridge, microwave, and TV for cash at the same time and thinking this all started withdrawing an eyebrow. Drawing an eyebrow paved the most beautiful path for me. Drawing an eyebrow gave me financial freedom. Drawing an eyebrow resulted in my ultimate success. I never take that for granted.

Chapter 10

THE PURPOSE BEHIND THE WORK

Being a makeup artist has given me platforms that I have never thought I would be at. Above all, being a makeup artist has given me the privilege to work with women from all walks of life. When I started my career because I had to stop going to church for a while, and when I went back, my Sundays were always fully booked, I struggled to find my place, how to worship God in service. So I realized with the women and men I work with from different backgrounds, going through different levels of life, and when I work, there is a point of ministry to offer. My background has, in a way, prepared me for many different struggles in life, be it be emotionally, spiritually, or economically. Sometimes someone wants someone who can listen to them, share a word of prayer with them, be it encouraging words or checking up on them now and again. There are relationships and friendships that are a form of discipleship that I have formed within my work environment.

There are instances when I get to a bride, and she is having a breakdown because of the pressure, nerves, and anxiety. We first address that, take a few minutes to share the word and minister peace. Everything is purposeful, God works through people, and he has made sure their mark serves a purpose to the next person. How are you of service to other people? This is important to live a more fulfilling life. At some point, I was working with a client who had a skin problem. She literally cried when she looked at herself in the mirror after I was done with her. She said, 'I didn't think I would look this good. That is where the fulfillment comes in for me. When I see different women genuinely pleased about my work, I am again reminded that I am aligned with my purpose.

I have seen an immediate switch in moods from clients. I have worked with clients who came in sad left really happy. I understand that doing my work is more than just drawing eyebrows. It is about transformation, it is about boosting confidence, and it is about building relationships.

Memorable client moments

I received a booking from the UK, and she was getting married in South Africa, and she was worried that if we didn't do a trial and that her skin, according to her, was hopeless and had some blemishes and scars, and zero hope that anything can be done about it, Luckily now I had some experience and on the wedding day I delivered, what I didn't expect was the reaction. Her sisters and her where wailing in joy, shock and excitement. After all she was going to walk down the aisle looking like a dream.

I was booked for a wedding by a client I had done a few times and had always been happy with my work. She came with the husband to be for a trial as they were doing their engagement shoot, and like always, she loved the look. After the shoot, I received a couple of messages from the bride to be that the fiancé had a different vision for the makeup for the wedding day, and it seemed like it contradicted to what she wanted, but for the sake of peace and obviously, she wanted to please her husband to be she was caught in between with a look to go for her big day. I remember going to the wedding, not sure which look I would go for, that is going suit her needs at the same make her feel like she also accommodated and honored her husband. I never do my clients in front of the mirror, so it was time for the big reveal when I had finished her makeup. It was waterworks, everyone in the room was crying, including me. I ended up excusing myself because I could not stop crying at that moment. I felt a rush of the anointing over my body, I had goosebumps, and my hairs were standing on end. I can't tell you whether the look I did was what she wanted or what her husband wanted, but I know everyone was happy about it, and I felt a confirmation from God that I called you for this. Now and again, you face difficult clients, doubt your abilities, encounter backlash with people saying there are too many makeup artists, you will not make it.

The scripture doesn't say all things are good, but it does say that all things WORK together for good for those that love the Lord. All I had to do was shut my ears, put in the work, and apply the positive principles. Negativism had to go and start thinking and speaking in agreement with His will and plan. There are many looks and clients I tried to get but failed; anytime we don't get what we want, our feelings will rise up and try to get us into self-pity and negative attitude. A negative person never enjoys anything; I had to let go of the negative to enjoy my career and life in general.

Chapter 11

THE NEXT STEP

The future holds many possibilities. I have understood my career requires me to be agile and consistently evolving. It is strongly attached to my personal growth as well. The beauty industry revolves around beauty and seeks to enhance your natural features by producing innovative products that should be safe to use. We have since manufactured our first cosmetic product; the eyelashes vary from mink and faux lash textures. Consumer satisfaction is paramount. We place a premium on making our customers happy hence we have more than 12 different styles of eyelashes. As a self-taught makeup artist, using my experience, I was able to bring about a product that is industry-appropriate for both personal and professional use. Our business plan is geared to maintain a loyal client base. Our products recognize the unique needs of individual customers from a dramatic look to a natural look. We will continue to thrive to offer safe products, quality packaging, a wide product range, and reasonable prices for all our current and future products.

I have had the opportunity to be a guest speaker in many prominent business workshops, most recently the one breakfast business with the Zimbabwean ambassador to South Africa. I had the opportunity to share my journey to entrepreneurship and lessons learned from my previous employment. We will continue to engage with other aspiring business owners, government and create a solid business network, especially among young people.

We have so far done more than ten beauty masterclasses between Zimbabwe and South Africa. The main objective of these skill development programs is to equip people with self-sustaining skills that can improve their financial status. Our Workshops are designed to improve one's personal and professional skills, focusing on communicating and engaging with potential clients, intensive exposure to the beauty industry, the skill required, and what to expect in the field. The masterclasses give access to the beauty experts in makeup artistry, hair, nail techs. It also allows the attendees to meet other people who share their interests and experiences, facilitating an exchange of ideas and perspectives. With the beauty industry consistently evolving, there is always a need to know how other artists find solutions to common problems and advice on handling different clients and products. Therefore, we will continue with these workshops and equip as many people as possible.

Elinah initiatives

It's our social responsibility to the community to share what God has blessed us with. We offer free masterclasses, sanitary wear, stationery, clothes. We have since done three charity beauty masterclasses in South Africa at a girl's home and sent a few tools like nappies. Fleeces, pins, needles, manilla scissors in Zimbabwe to facilitate a training program where girls can sow together their re-usable pads (Mentoring and counseling programs are present). We see the demonstration of giving in the word of God, *1ˢᵗ Cor 16 vs2 "every Sunday, each of you make a generous offering by taking a portion of whatever God has blessed you with and place it in safekeeping. Then I won't have to make a special appeal when I come. When I arrive, I will send your gift to the poor in Jerusalem along with a letter of explanation, carried by those whom you approve.* We are encouraged to set aside an amount of money to give each week; it is about reaching out to the community and bringing about effective change.

Skills development

If you make you a better you but it goes no further than you, you are nothing more than an annoying version of you; Maya Angelou says when you learn, you teach, then you get given. With this, I was strongly motivated to create a skills development program where I host masterclasses to provide skills and information for any makeup artist, whether aspiring or professional, to groom and sharpen their skill. The Beauty masterclasses offer valuable performance opportunities to gain fresh ideas on makeup trends, new products, techniques, business strategies and to make contact with high production companies, campaigns, brands, and models. The masterclasses are recommended for beginners and professionals alike. These are also available on a one-on-one basis.

I also run an NPO called ELINAH INITIATIVES, which offers free beauty masterclasses and a mentorship program at girls' homes. Our focus is to donate sanitary wear and free beauty masterclasses to girls' homes in and around Johannesburg. The objective is to equip them with life skills that will bring financial independence, motivate them to study and pursue their careers of choice. We currently have 25 girls between the age of 12 years–19 years; due to different circumstances of abuse, rape, junkie parents, and orphaned they end up in the home. There is a great need for mentorship and counseling for them to deal with past traumas and how to create a different, better future for themselves. I believe God has much more for them "You pick up the poor of the dirt, rescue the wretched who've been thrown out with the trash, Seats them among the honored guest.

I am consistently asked how do I keep positive and maintain my posture; it's all on the daily habits we develop and nature. When the bible in *Isaiah 40 vs 31, "but those who hope in the Lord will renew their strength, they will soar on wings like eagles, they will run and not grow weary, they will walk and not faint ..* ' and in *Psalms 92 vs 13 planted in the house of the Lord, they will flourish in the courts of God, (growing grace) they will still thrive and bear fruit and prosper, they will flourish and be vital and fresh (rich in trust and love and contentment)*

I have since learned that if I hope, stay connected, and be planted in the house of the Lord, I will continually be refreshed, and the more I give, the more is given back.

I would say that this has been a transforming journey for me, too, from a tomboy who knew nothing about makeup to one of the baddest self-taught Makeup artists in the streets. It has helped me shape my personality, understand other people better, what it means to be in a relationship with God. God doesn't make a mistake; everything you have gone, been through, and going to go through serves a purpose, embrace it. Everything is Purposeful.

I am Elinah 'Success' Mangena, and the journey continues...

#friends #prayerpartners #zimgirls

8 July

aynie_jay So insomnia hit me n been watching your tutorials for hours now then decided to come here then I realized I have screenshots from WhatsApp when a friend of mine Mantate posted you .. you're definitely booked for my wedding 😭😂

6h   1 like   Reply

elinah_mangena @aynie_jay hey mamie ... this time insomnia served us well 🙈🙈 thank you so much for watching the videos 🐥🐥🐥🐥 siyashadisa 🤍 I will be there and ready ,

Just watched your YouTube video on how to be a make-up artist n how to start as a beginner including the challenges faced .

After watching that video I can say I'm inspired, bczi was scared and didn't know whr to start ..... I'm saying all this bczi loved make-up n I always wished to be a make-up artist of which I have started taking my chances on being a make-up artist. Start small because I'm still a student and can't afford much products .

So all I wnt to say it's because of you tht I managed to open up an account to showcase n see wt Will happen . Thanks you so much sis 🤍 💋

My make-up skills are not perfect as of yet but they are not bad .... I watch your make-up videos most of the times to help myself improve...... As time goes I will apply for a

◎ Message...   🎤 🖼 ➕

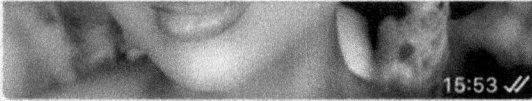

15:53 ✓✓

15:53 ✓✓

Today

elinah i can't thank you enough   10:17

everyone complimented my makeup. you did an exceptional job🖤   10:18

thank you   10:18

as soon as i receive the professional photos. i will tag you and send you some   10:18

\+   🖼 ☐ 🎤

09:55

1182   10:35

18:19 ✓✓

18:22 ✓✓

18:22 ✓✓

18:22 ✓✓

You were really amazing. I like your personality, and your amazing work !! Keep it up sisi May God bless you

18:23

< ⬤ **neilfacebeats** ▢ ⚐ ⓘ

View Profile

Yesterday at 11:02

You are a great inspiration to me , I wanna be like you
Everytime when m at lowest , I just watch ur igtv , n be fine , everything you say makes sense to me , m going through a lot , n your words always encourage me to do better , I pray that you get blessed more than this
You really touch my life n I know one day I will be a makeup artist like you

◉ Hun| Send

In   Uhm   It

q w e r t y u i o p

a s d f g h j k l

⇧ z x c v b n m ⌫

123 😀 🎤   space   return

<   **tinomidzi_photogr...**
Active now

tinomidzi_photography

Instagram

2K followers · 52 posts

You follow each other on Instagram

You both follow samantha_the_mua and 40 others

View Profile

8:06 am

I have been scrolling up and down your account. Your makeup is absolutely amazing.

It can make any photographer better 👏 👏 👏 👏

Message...

Nosihle Ngubane
nosihle_n_

10:54 pm

Girl do you see God though? I'm still surprised that that live didn't cut anywho thoroughly enjoyed it and stop don't. I'm rooting for you as an aspiring makeup artist myself. You got this beautiful 🤍

Bathong so many typos but I'm sure you get it 😂 on that note can I please volunteer to be the lady that attends the master class for free. 🙈

Girl girl you came through for me 😫😫😫😫😫 like thank you so so much for this kind love hun !! Trust me it's not going to waste .... I don't even know how this live went for 2hrs 30 mins without cutting

Hahahah Wena you deserve it njani ... I will keep that in mind , you might come as my assistant, am watching nje

Message...

Only you can
see this

🔥
🤍

Yesterday at 4:42 pm

Hey hun thank you soo much for the
tips on how to grow your make up
business I really learnt soo much and
things I was taking granted for and u
highlighted them so clearly!I have
taken note ✅ thanks boss lady your
make up is on point and I noticed it
took nothing but practice everyday
👏 I went through your tutorials I'm
on YouTube and I want to try them
out...um so motivated gurllll and
inspired by your journey
Keep up the good work

1:26 am

Message...   🎤 🖼 ➕

Sliyonce
Active 6h ago

Saturday 8:50 am

Replied to your story

Only you can
see this

Amen!

Monday 9:38 am

I just love u, and pray dat u get more
subscribers on YouTube coz wow ur
work, 1 day I need a 1 on 1 makeup
session . Stay blessed .

Double-tap to like

Yesterday at 4:24 am

This humbles my soul , and I know
God is faithful in all of his ways ... I
will be here waiting for you sis 😍

Message...

30 May, 6:53 am

Replied to your story

Only you can
see this

Woke up and binged watched all your
vids.You are definitely that girl that
you think you are 🖤 You are very
good at what you do I pray you get
the recognition in the industry

Double-tap to like

31 May, 1:46 am

Hey Oyama, thank you so so much
for your consistent support and
encouragement and oh watching my
videos 😍😍😍😍. Oh your kind
words humble me so so much

Message...

Okay 👌

Yesterday

Hey there am outside

Morning
Ok   08:33

What's the name of the complex

▶ ● ━━━━━━━━━━━━━━
0:03   08:34 🎙

Unit

Should I wait at the gate or ?

Thank you so much for coming through.
I cant seem to put the mirror down. Your
work is super phenomenal. May your cup
be filled beyond measure.   10:33

WHAT IT TAKES TO BE A SEASONED BEAUTY MAESTRO!

21st Century Skills or transferable skills are a list of abilities anyone needs to succeed at school, in their future jobs, and in everyday life, the Acer P21 Framework for 21st Century Learning, the skills can be divided into three areas,

1. ***Learning and Innovation Skills*** are those skills that separate students who will be able to deal with an increasingly complex society in the 21st century: critical thinking, creative thinking, collaboration, and communication.

2. ***Information Media and Technology Skills.***
In a society based on technology and media, we must learn how to properly use them in order to be able to evaluate the abundance of information we get into contact with, becoming attentive citizens and workers. The skills to develop are information Literacy, Media Literacy, Technology Literacy.

3. ***Life and Careers Skills***
To deal with complex life and work environment's we need to develop thinking skills, content knowledge, social and emotional competencies like flexibility, initiative, social skills, productivity, and leadership.

Makeup Artistry falls under creativity; Everyone has a creative side; they just might not know it yet. Creativity is the use of imagination or original ideas to create something, inventiveness. We are in an era where one requires and develops a personality channeled to bring income. The Covid pandemic has proven to us that one requires multiple streams of income, and we need to invest in ourselves by continuously adding new skills. We have since seen a vast number of professionals retrenched and brawl for the same job in the job market.

If you are an aspiring Makeup Artist and you desire to be the best in the game, here are some hacks and tricks you can use to develop your skill, remain consistent, grow your reach and manage your time, and remain motivated.

Five ways to become a makeup artist without going to make-up school

1. *Do your Research*
In any career that you want to venture into, It's essential that you do extensive research on it so that you understand what the industry is about. Watch tons of online videos to understand what the skill is about and how much work and time is required to do what you need to do. Also, research if you can make money in this industry or in your own area. Some cities are busier than other cities.

2. *Self-reflect*
You need to dig deep within yourself if you have the personality traits required for you to become a makeup artist because you will be working with a lot of different people from different places and cultures. E.g., if you are shy or timid, you might need to address this area as working with people will require a certain level of boldness and assertiveness.

3. *Practice*
After doing research and self-reflection, it comes down to the skill.

You need to practice. Les Brown says, *"Everything we do is practice for something greater than where we currently are; practice only makes for improvement,"* This is a creative skill to be a master of one; we need to do it over and over again. However, don't put yourself under pressure when trying looks, and they don't' come out immediately as you expected. Be patient with yourself and practice as long as you do better than you did the last try. It's always better to practice on other people than yourself; you don't want to be a makeup artist that is good at doing themselves but can't do other people. You will eventually get it right. Start with basic looks and then move slowly to advanced looks.

4. Look for gigs

Approach businesses and volunteer in makeup stores because being there will expose you to different types of skin and face shapes. This gives you an opportunity to learn in a short space of time and compels you to do your research. This will also help will also improve your people skills, how to interact with them, and do pleasing work. You can then use this platform to start building your market, that after your period as a volunteer, you had earned a good market base that trusts you and has confidence in your skill.

5. Find a mentor

A mentor can help you focus your efforts by setting goals and giving feedback.

Look for a makeup artist that does what you really want to do or know and request to shadow them. They serve as a source of knowledge, help make connections in the industry, offer encouragement. Volunteer to assist them, e.g., through washing their brushes or carrying their bags, any admin work required. That's how you get first-hand experience on how to become a makeup artist. You will get to learn how they handle their clients and how they deal with different types of shoots, i.e., bridal, corporate, etc., products and tools they use, and where you purchase some. Yes, some will require you to pay them for mentorship, but it's generally affordable and worth it considering the knowledge attained.

Bonus Point

● *Build your portfolio*

When all is said and done, start creating your portfolio depending on the makeup artistry that you want to pick. Invest in a good phone, good lighting, and take quality pictures so that when someone sees your work, they are really interested in working with you. We are living in a digital era, visuals are important, how you portray your work on Instagram is important, it must be appealing and attractive to the potential client. Also, invest in your social media because it will be your greatest marketing tool.

How to grow your business as a freelance makeup artist

Tips on how to grow your client base

1. Make sure that your skill is perfect

Ensure that your work is quality regardless of what your client is paying you, regardless of what you are feeling on that day or how the client receives you. Don't let emotions come between you and the work that you produce. Your client is your most significant source of referral. Commit at all times to deliver quality work

2. Customer Service

Sell your personality. It's been proven that people are attracted and buy-in emotion and feeling. People will never forget how you made them feel. When you are with your clients, you want to make them comfortable. You want to make them relate to you, so that is a comfortable flow of communication. Every client is different, and you need to serve them as best as you can, even the most challenging clients. If you meet a challenging client, e.g., they are not in a good mood, you need to find a way to cheer them up. Believe me; they will be grateful for that. Ben Cohen says, *"There is a spiritual aspect to our lives, when we give, when a business does something good for somebody, that somebody feels good about them".*

3. Punctuality
Some say punctuality is the soul of business. Always be on time. If they say 14:00, be there at 13:50 so that you have time to set up. You'd rather wait for the client. Punctuality also gives you time to create the kind of work that you want to create. You don't want the uncles at the door screaming that the bride is late; that puts you under pressure and eventually compromises the quality of your work, and you never want to compromise your brand name.

4. Professionalism
Make sure you arrive there looking spot on. Make sure you sanitize your hands. Make sure your brushes are clean. Make sure your kit is clean. Make sure that you have a cap to cover your client. It's very important that you travel with your own chair. Communicate kindly with the client and the people around the client. Communicate should you be late for any reason. Be always kind and thoughtful, "Scott Adams remember there is no such thing as a small act of kindness. Every act creates a ripple with no logical end.

5. Pictures
Makeup artistry is a visual work; what you put out is very important. When you post pictures, don't use a lot of filters or photoshop a lot. This may compromise your business in a way that if what you post and what you actually do on a client is completely different will cause tension between you and the clients. Learn how to produce a flawless look without a lot of edits. Clients will really appreciate that.

6. Post on social media
We live in a digital era. Make sure you have a strong digital footprint. Schedule social media posting in your business plan. Use the Instagram and Facebook business tools. Be consistent in your posting; make your brand known and visible. With social media, you are able to reach a wider market outside your circle. Post every day, both on your timeline and stories.

7. Support other businesses
It's more like networking. If I support you, it becomes easy for you to support me. Creating great networks is amazing. Networking allows you access to opportunities you might not be able to find on your own. It will also give you an insight into new beauty trends, different products and tools, and generally how to improve professionally.

8. Be confident
Approach the people and businesses you want to work with because you never know whose door you are knocking at and might just open for you. Don't be scared to propose mutually beneficial collaborations. Understanding your potential and capacity might be what you need to get to your next level.

9. Know your target Market
Know who you want to work with. Market yourself to your target market. At times we are scared to charge what we are worth in fear of losing clients, but charging less means going for cheaper brands that might affect the quality of work produced. If anyone complains that you are expensive, they are not your target market. Analyze your services, and it will help you know "who who's" that are likely to purchase the product.

10. Social media mentions
Kindly ask your clients to tag you, mention you on social media, and

reshare your work. It's basically your clients endorsing your work, and nothing beats a referral.

The truths that Makeup artists want you to know!

Being a Makeup Artist comes with its Pros and cons.

The Cons
- ***You need to crawl before you walk***
It's going to take some time to build a client base, be known, and get bookings. It will take a number of tries before you become a commendable makeup artist. Be patient, though.

- ***Time limits***
Sometimes you can be punctual, but the client is late. Then now, you have limited time to execute your task. This creates a ripple effect and can cause you to be late to your following clients.

- ***Pricing***
There will be clients that will always mention that other makeup artists charge lower rates. Do not succumb to this pressure. Put into account your product range, time, and skill as well and value accordingly.

- ***Makeup artists don't have Fridays.***
Most makeup artists don't have Fridays because most of our Saturdays are early mornings and long days. We need to prepare the night before and sleep early to wake up refreshed and ready for a long working Saturday.

- ***Friends and family freebies***
Friends, family, and colleagues will always want to do their makeup for free every time. For all family events, be cautious not to bring your makeup kit, it might result in you doing everyone's

makeup and using up all your products, and it can be exhausting. Rather have family rates.

- ### *We don't have off days.*
As a freelance makeup artist, you can get a call for a gig at any time, and every cent counts; you are not certain when you can get another client again. So, never complain because being busy means you are making money. However, as you get busier, it's important to allocate a day of rest to avoid burnout.

- ### *Free consultation*
Responding to people's questions about makeup on social media DMs can be very overwhelming.

The Pros
- ### *Money*
Being a makeup artist can pay really well, especially if you have established your client base and your skill is great. Clients are willing to pay whatever the cost may be as long as it is worth it.

- ### *Being your own boss*
You can decide which client you want to work with, and you have the freedom to manage your own time. You have a greater sense of satisfaction; you have an open-ended career progression your income is limited only by your own willpower and proficiency. You will have higher motivation and morale because you are aware of the benefits of the work you put in.

- ### *It's rewarding*
One of the reasons why I decided to make makeup artistry beautiful is that it is very rewarding. I love making women beautiful. There is nothing more rewarding than seeing a happy client's reaction after doing their makeup.

● **Opportunities to travel**
You get to travel at a client's cost. Flight booked, accommodation booked, and food expenses covered. It's like getting a free holiday.

● **You learn a lot**
You learn a lot because you are going to different events. With the mere fact that you are there as a makeup artist, you get to have access to events that may positively impact your life. Someone once said, *"it is not your qualifications but your exposure in life that makes you who you are."*

● **It's fun**
Most of the time, it never really feels like work. Different occasions, different people, different atmosphere, you are moving from a production shoot to a wedding to a 21st birthday party to a graduation to a photoshoot, its consistently high spirit occasions and you get to have the front seat of them all.

Different clients, you meet as a Makeup artist
Different workspaces mean different clients.

1. *The staring client*
This client looks at you straight in the eyes while you are working on their face. It can either be uncomfortable or funny.

2. *The picky client*
This client is very particular. You will probably spend more time than you normally would when working with this client as a makeup. However, you would still need to be patient with this client because makeup artistry is a service job.

3. *The Quiet Client*
This client makes you wonder if they are happy or if you are doing

the right thing. However, some clients like being quiet, so you need to be understanding of that.

4. Undecided client
This client is not sure what they want, and it can be a bit confusing. They want a natural look with an eye look that stands out or a glam look, but that is natural, lol. You can assist the client by finding out what kind of an outfit they are wearing, which event they are going to, and making a suggestion.

5. The "do you" clients
This is my favorite client. This client gives you the freedom to exercise your creativity on a high level. However, you must trust your skills when a client says, "do you." You must know the type of event they are going to and the outfit they will probably wear and combine with their personality.

6. The first-time make-up client.
This client has never had their make-up done before, either by a professional or themselves. So they are worried and excited at the same time. They can get easily overwhelmed. You need to make them comfortable and assure them that you will take care of them.

7. The busy client
They are on the phone. They are easily distracted. Sometimes they want to eat. Working on these dynamics can be quite tricky, but it can be done.

As much as there are different types of clients, quality work can still be produced in those different dynamics. Always be prepared, communicate well with your clients, and be professional.

What's inside a beginners makeup kit

I always share this statement with my students every time. (WHEN YOU CAN UNDERSTAND WHY YOU ARE DOING WHAT YOU ARE DOING, IT WILL HELP YOU KNOW WHAT PRODUCT TO USE, WHERE TO APPLY IT AND WHICH TOOL USE TO APPLY IT), when you figure this out, you have mastered the game of makeup artistry; you can quote me on that.

- Facial wipes (Clicks)

Wipes remove 99% of makeup. They are a quick and easy alternative to take off makeup without water or a cleanser. Facial wipes are convenient, they can easily be carried around and be used anytime., but they must never replace washing your face daily, especially after having your makeup on.

- Cotton pads (Clicks)

These have many purposes and are used across many industries, from medical to cosmetics. In addition, they have multiple uses: applying toner, removing makeup with micellar, or cleansing water.

- Primer (LA Girl Primer)

It's a preparatory product applied after your skincare to create an ideal canvas to hold onto whatever makeup comes afterward.

- Serum (essence)

They are perfect for different kinds of skin types whether, dry, oily wrinkled, etc. they tend to penetrate the skin more and effectively than moisturizers)

- Foundation Shades to start with (kryolan D13, D13L, D13/14, D13/14LL, D16)

I can talk about this foundation from the moon and back; it's basically my fighter. It was my concealer for eyebrows, highlight, and contouring when I started it out.

- Can cover heavy discolorations, scarring, etc.
- Waterproof
- Contains SPF
- Sweat-resistant
- Can be used for both matte or dewy finish.
- Long-lasting effect

- Concealer (Fawn, Cool Tan, Porcelain, Expresso, Natural)
Means to conceal; we conceal dark spots, dark circles, blemishes, or any kind of pigmentations.

- Eyeshadows (The color board, Jaclyn Hill)
This is where all the makeup is at; it makes the eyes stand out and look more attractive. I at times use it as blush or bronzer.

- Brush set (face and eye brushes)(@esmangena))
Your number 1 tool, brushes, are for application for products like foundation, concealer, eyeshadows, etc.

- Powder (Kryolan P5, TL4) Compact Powder (essence)
Powder helps to set concealer and foundation so that it does slide off your face or create lines. It also helps to absorb any excess oil from your foundation or concealer; some powders can be used for coverage and are a great base for blush and bronzer application.

- Setting spray (LA Girl)
These help to lock and keep your makeup intact, and they extend the longevity of your makeup look. They also avoid and reduce makeup transfer to your clothes.

- Eyebrow pencil (essence No2)

It's used to fill in your eyebrows and bring more definition and color
- Lipstick (L'Oréal)

The purpose has always remained the same to express yourself, add color, and protect your lips.

- Lip liner (Mac Chestnut)

Lipliners are important. They prevent your lipstick from bleeding to outline your lips to make them look plummy and fuller.

- Bronzer (Huda Beauty)

It creates a depression on your cheeks, jawline, and hairline, resulting in a more chiseled face.

- Blush (Mac)

Bring color and make your complexion look healthier, brighter, and glowy.

- Eyelashes (@esmangena)

Our natural eyelashes serve an actual function, to keep dirt out of your eyes; false eyelashes finish the look perfectly and enhance your eye makeup.

- Razor blades (Gillette) Tweezer (Clicks)

To trim and clean up your eye makeup or any facial hair that might be in the way of your makeup process.

- Eyelashes scissors (Clicks)

To resize your eyelash stripe depending on the size of the eye.

I hope that this will kick start your career as a professional makeup artist and for some encourage you to try out makeup for personal use to just beautify yourself.

CONTACT THE AUTHOR

We would like to hear from you, share with us your Testimonies and let us know how we can help you work on yourself or for receiving more Products from the Author.

Cell no: +27 81 235 0684

Email address: epnmangena@gmail.com

Facebook page: @thebossladylook

Instagram: @esmangena

Twitter: @Elinah Mangena

Do you have a dream, a passion to write books?

Get in touch with us

We are ready to review your manuscript and

Help you make your dream successful.

+27 72 931 6810

tich@drtich.com

www.drtich.com

www.ingramcontent.com/pod-product-compliance
Lightning Source LLC
Chambersburg PA
CBHW071232090426
42736CB00014B/3053